Advance Praise

"This delightful and inspiring work recounts an important and forever altering time in the author's life. Yet the work is more than a series of events; it's an eye-opening experience for the author and the reader as both ponder the lessons extracted from life and children in Thailand. Seidel offers readers a new and unique perspective on life and life lessons found in the unlikeliest of places and moments."

> — The BookLife Prize

"As an educator, *Kindergarten at 60: A Memoir of Teaching in Thailand* spoke to my heart. I found myself picturing doing something similar in my retirement days. This book showcases a strong and courageous woman who refuses to let life's obstacles stand in the way of her dreams."

> — *Midwest Book Review*

"Former climate scientist Dian Seidel chronicles her revelations as she and her husband Steve teach kindergarten in Thailand. While realizing that life past 60 is full of adventures, they try to embrace the Thai philosophy of *mai pen rai*, or relax and enjoy what life brings. This well-written travelogue will appeal particularly to people looking forward to the next chapter of their lives."

> — Blythe Grossberg, Psy.D., author of *I Left My Homework in the Hamptons*

"In bite-size chapters, Dian Seidel gives her readers a bouquet of adventures in modern Thailand, putting before us a savory feast of small revelations and daily obstacles that transform into moments of compassion and joy."

> — Virginia Hartman, author of *The Marsh Queen*

"Dian Seidel turned the page on an eminent career in climate science to embark on a completely different pursuit: teaching English to children in Thailand. There is a wisdom and warmth here in discovering adventure at an age   ple's vocabularies. They say learning a language stretches the mind. What happens when that is combined with immersion in a completely different culture on the other side of the world? Seidel presents her adventure in a series of vignettes, seeing big picture issues through the lens of a kindergarten classroom. She emerges from her trial with strength and grace and gentleness."

> — David Goodrich, author of *A Hole in the Wind: A Climate Scientist's Bicycle Journey Across the United States*

"A charming tale of a second act and self-discovery in a far-off tropical clime. Dian Seidel did what the rest of us only talk about."

> — John Burgess, author of *Angkor's Temples in the Modern Era: War, Pride, and Tourist Dollars*

"Dian Seidel gives us a delightful glimpse into Thailand and its culture, reminding us that we can find adventure in post-retirement years. Her memoir brings to life the commonalities of children around the world and the struggles of teachers everywhere."

> — Sarah Birnbach, author of *A Daughter's Kaddish: My Year of Grief, Devotion, and Healing*

"When it's time to retire from a structured life, what do you do? In Dian Seidel's book, *Kindergarten at 60*, she invites you to join her and her husband in their voyage into the unknown language, culture, history and social values of Thailand. *Kindergarten at 60* is an interesting mix of the challenges and adventure they find along with the heartwarming discovery of the children and fellow international teachers they bond with during their stay."

> — Tom Crowley, author *Mercy's Heroes* and *Bangkok Gamble*.

"*Kindergarten at 60* is a beautifully written memoir with the perfect touch of humor. It is a joy to join Dian Seidel on her five-month assignment teaching children in Pathum Thani, a place far from home. Simultaneously teacher and student, she learns valuable lessons about herself from her young Thai students. The heart of *Kindergarten at 60* is an endearing love story of a retired couple enjoying the adventure together. Thank you, Teacher Dian for taking us on this journey. *Khop khun kha.*"

> — Michelle Paris, author of *New Normal*

"A heartwarming, informative and inspiring memoir about our ability to learn at any age through our willingness to serve and open our hearts to the new and unexpected."

> — Nina Wise, performance artist

Kindergarten at 60

Kindergarten at 60

A Memoir of Teaching in Thailand

Dian Seidel

Apprentice
House Press
Loyola University Maryland

First Edition

Library of Congress Control Number: 2022949962

Hardcover ISBN: 978-1-62720-445-3
Paperback ISBN: 978-1-62720-446-0
Ebook ISBN: 978-1-62720-447-7

Author photo by Derek Parks
Internal & cover design by April Hartman
Map design by Sienna Whalen
Editorial development by Cat Cusma
Promotional development by Brett Duffy

Published by Apprentice House Press

Apprentice
House Press
Loyola University Maryland

Loyola University Maryland
4501 N. Charles Street, Baltimore, MD 21210
410.617.5265
www.ApprenticeHouse.com
info@ApprenticeHouse.com

To Teacher Steve. Khop khun kha.
I couldn't have done it, any of it, without you.

Contents

Author's Note

Call me Teacher Dian. That's what they called me at the school in Thailand where my husband, Teacher Steve, and I taught kindergarten.

Most foreign English teachers in Thailand are young adults, fresh out of school. We were retirees. Like our younger colleagues, we went to Thailand seeking adventure. But we also went with some trepidation and with little understanding of the country.

We encountered a culture, a language, an educational system, and a climate very different from what we knew. We tried to figure things out, adapted when we could, and did our best not to sweat the small stuff. Our experience was both an adventure and an education—about Thailand and about ourselves.

Much about Thailand still remains a mystery to me, and I take responsibility for any errors of fact or interpretation in this book. Almost all of the dialogue is reimagined, because, apart from a few choice turns of phrase, I don't remember the details of conversations.

Respecting the privacy of our family, friends, colleagues, and students, I have changed most of their names as well as those of our school and some businesses. A glossary of Thai and other foreign-language words is at the back of this book.

• • •

Lyrics from *The Swim Song* © Nina Wise, 1988, are used in the chapter "Buoyant Memory" with the songwriter's permission.

Excerpts of this memoir have previously been published in *Passager* (no. 70, Winter 2021), *Anak Sastra* (no. 46, February 2022), *Lucky Jefferson* (no. 9, 2022), and *Bethesda Magazine* (Vol. 19, no. 4, July/August 2022).

First Morning Chorus

Our class looks like a pint-sized platoon preparing to march forward to face the day. The children stand, arm's distance apart, toes lined up on a seam in the playground's artificial turf, facing their teachers. Each kindergartner is in uniform—blue shirt and plaid shorts or skirt. Each shirt has a child's name embroidered on the right breast, which will make our first day at Pathum Thani Prep a little easier. Some stare, some smile shyly, at Steve and me, their new teachers. Eleven orderly children in the care of four teachers. How hard could this be?

Head Teacher Miranda calls, "Ivy and Panit, come to the flagpole." A tallish girl with long braids and a stout, round-faced boy scamper forward and excitedly reach up to take the rope. The sun, an orange disc still low in the hazy gray sky, is already hot. Rivulets of perspiration run down the boy's temples and the groove of my own spine. Miranda wheels out a suitcase-sized boombox and plays a recording of the Thai national anthem. It is eight o'clock on an October morning in 2019, and at this moment similar scenes are unfolding at schools across the Kingdom of Thailand, where loyalty to country and monarch is taught from birth.

The opening chords bring the children to attention as all eyes focus on the red, white, and blue striped flag rising up the pole. Ivy and the older children know most of the words, while the younger ones, including two-year-old Panit, sway and nod in time with the music.

Miranda looks at the nodders with an expression—accessible only to a master kindergarten teacher—that combines sternness, support, and affection in perfect proportions. She throws her shoulders back and holds her head still in an effort to encourage the children to do the same. Most get the message, but she needs to place her hands on Panit's shoulders to straighten his back. Will standing at attention suffice for Steve and me? Or will we need to sing like the older kids? I make a mental note to find a transliteration of the words to the anthem and wonder if I'll ever master that look of Miranda's that so completely commands the children's respect.

The next song is also in Thai. Based on the rousing chorus and the repetition of the only Thai words I recognize in the lyrics, our school's name, this must be its alma mater song.

Steve's eyebrows rise and jaw drops, and I try to mask my own amazement and concern. According to Miranda's schedule, next week we will be responsible for morning assembly. How will we learn these songs and whatever others come next? Will we rely on four-year-old Ivy to lead the singing?

But the next number boosts our confidence. *Baby shark, doo, doo, doo, doo, doo, doo!* Who would have guessed that being baseball fans would be good training for morning assembly at Pathum Thani Prep? Inexplicably, the Washington Nationals, our hometown team, have adopted *Baby Shark* as a rallying song, so we have the lyrics and hand gestures down pat. It's a catchy little tune—actually, too catchy. It will stick in my head all day. And many days to come.

The next few songs are in English, too. Learning lyrics won't be tough, but each one is choreographed, with complicated hand gestures that put *Baby Shark* in a category with "peek-a-boo-I-see-you." A favorite seems to be *Let's Do the Pinocchio*, a body parts vocabulary builder that has the children dancing around like marionettes. Most of the kids know the steps and gestures better than the lyrics. Ivy knows them all by heart.

Miranda plays one last song. A slow, sweet melody fills the air, and on this cue all the children sit down. Their posture is impressive—no one is slouching, and their little legs are folded into beautiful lotus poses. The music swells, and the children take in a deep, audible breath. Their hands move as if to guide the air toward their faces, which grow visibly calmer as they sing.

I'm breathing in
I'm breathing out
As flowers bloom
Eleven pairs of hands form petals, slowly rotate, and rise.
The mountains high
The rivers sigh
The air that I breathe
I fly

I watch chests rise and fall with alternating lines of the song as the verse repeats. At an instrumental interlude, the children gently cover their faces and turn their gazes inward. The gesture brings a flash of memory from my childhood: my grandmother is covering her face while chanting the blessing over glowing Sabbath candles. This moment in the sun on the playground seems almost as sacred.

Miranda has the children line up to go inside, but despite the turf seam as a guide, our platoon breaks ranks. Panit runs ahead to the classroom door, and Steve dashes to catch him.

A soft breeze gently lifts the Thai flag and brings a momentary floral fragrance, delicate and peachlike. A little finger taps the back of my hand. It is Ivy, looking up at me with curiosity.

"Hello, Ivy," I say. "You like singing, don't you?"

"Oh, yes, I do, doo, doo, doo, doo, doo," she assures me.

"Me too," I tell her. And I like this morning ritual and the eager anticipation in this girl's eyes.

I take Ivy's hand. "What a great way to start our day!"

Why Thailand?

How did I, at age sixty and with no background in early childhood education, find myself a rookie kindergarten teacher in Pathum Thani, Thailand? Thailand was not my top choice for a postretirement destination, but that was when I thought we *had* choices.

• • •

"Close your eyes and spin the globe. Any place your finger lands is a possibility!" Paulette, our training program director, is positive we will easily find jobs. Having survived Paulette's intensive four-week course in February 2019, my husband, Steve, and I now have internationally recognized certifications and a jam-packed toolkit of techniques for teaching English for Speakers of Other Languages.

"With your volunteer ESOL teaching experience, university degrees, and successful careers, schools will scoop you up in a heartbeat," Paulette says. "Most other applicants have much shorter résumés."

If our training program classmates are a representative sample, other applicants' résumés are shorter because their *lives* are shorter. Looking around the room, it's obvious that we were working professionals and parents before they were even born.

Focusing on work and family for the past three decades, Steve and I have lived in exactly two places—first, Washington,

DC, and later, just five miles away in Maryland. Now in retirement, it's time to experience someplace completely different. But where?

A socially conscious friend suggests Laos or Vietnam, where speaking English can open doors to a decent job, a better life. "Do your part to make up for the devastation the US caused during the war," she argues, ticking off land mines, Agent Orange, abandoned Amerasian children.

The idealist in me is intrigued, but Steve balks, pointing out my tendency to wilt in tropical climates. "Hell no, she won't go," he proclaims in the antiwar protest cadence of his youth. Then, less stridently and more sympathetically, "Girl can't take the heat."

Intrigued by Chinese culture, Steve learns that China needs tens of thousands of English teachers. But an initial investigation reveals what might as well be a second Great Wall of China—national mandatory retirement at age fifty-five for women and sixty for men. We're both too old to get work visas. Steve is disappointed, but I'm relieved that we won't have to study Chinese, a tonal language best learned in childhood, not as a senior citizen.

Reading my mind, as she often does, my sister Nancy suggests, "How about somewhere you can speak the language? Like Italy, maybe?" Nancy, a kindergarten teacher's assistant, adores all things Italian. For the past four years, she and I have been spending her spring vacations in Italy, taking Italian lessons and indulging in art, espresso, pasta, and gelato. What a dream it would be to teach English at work and speak the world's most beautiful language the rest of the day.

"Sounds good to me," Steve chimes in, which causes a pang of guilt about my getaways with Nancy. But with just a little research we learn that Italy is not an option for us, either.

Without EU passports, we can't work in Europe.

Missed culinary opportunities aside, our passport problem is actually somewhat fortunate. I'm not looking for an *Eat, Pray, Love* tour. For me, the operative verb is *teach*. Western Europeans have ample opportunity to learn English. I want to go someplace where resources for language education are limited.

Eastern Europe would better fit that bill. Steve and I both feel a vague ancestral pull from "the old country," *shtetls* that our great-grandparents fled in the early twentieth century. But the openings we find in these former Soviet republics require a two-year contract, and we are unwilling to leave my ninety-five-year-old mother for so long a stint, so far away.

"You have issues with every country," our daughter Rose wryly observes. "Why not just stick with teaching ESOL here in Washington? Besides, these teach-English-abroad gigs are geared toward people my age, not yours."

"You may have a point about the age thing," Steve says, "but your mother really wants an overseas adventure."

He's right. I have loved my ESOL students, adult immigrants from almost every continent, working hard to learn a new language and make a new life. Their stories of their homelands, dreams for the future, and fresh perspectives on life in America awake in me a longing to see the world. But not as a tourist.

Over the years, Steve and I have traveled some, on vacation and for work, but we've never stayed away more than a few weeks. The adventure I want now, and that I've managed to convince Steve that he wants too, is to live in a different culture and get to know it. To eat, shop, work, and play like the locals do. To be part of a community and make a contribution.

"An adventure? Mom?" Rose snorts. "Yeah, an adventure with fancy coffee shops and yoga studios. I mean, whatever makes you feel good about yourself…"

"Don't worry," I interrupt, though I admit I may be the most risk-averse, comfort-loving person on the planet. "I'm sure we can step outside my comfort zone and still find a decent cup of coffee."

By April, we have a list of five countries, including several with celebrated café cultures: Argentina, Chile, Costa Rica, Malta, and Morocco. For the first time since we began our professional careers decades ago, we prepare résumés, take head shots, and line up references. We apply for openings at language schools, universities, and high schools.

Then we wait. We land one phone interview, with a school in Santiago. Carlos promises he will be in touch soon with offers for both of us.

Weeks go by with no word from Carlos or anyone else. Was Paulette's assessment of our marketability way off base, or were we duped? To be fair, her job was to train us as teachers, not to find us teaching posts. I can't help suspect that ageism is at work, though Steve wonders whether we'd have better luck if we weren't retired US government employees, especially in countries where Americans haven't always advanced the common good. Regardless of the reason, we need a Plan B.

In May, we contact Teach the World Travel, a US-based placement service. Working with overseas partners, and for a hefty fee, they guarantee a teaching job and help with visas, insurance, travel, and housing. We like the guarantee. And we like Kelsey, who is responsive, upbeat, and confident she can find a workaround to the program's age restrictions.

"I have good news and bad news," Kelsey says after speaking with her contacts abroad. "For all the countries on your list, the age limits are strict. But have you considered Thailand? My colleague there is certain he can find jobs for you."

Thailand. We honeymooned there. We have memories, some vivid, some vague. Touring Bangkok to see the Golden Buddha, the Emerald Buddha, and the Reclining Buddha, and passing thousands of other Buddhas every day. The all-purpose greeting *sawaddee* and the accompanying *wai* gesture—palms joined at the chest, head bowed. The melody of the Loy Krathong song for the autumn full moon holiday, an earworm even after all these years. Sweet, strong iced coffee that became a daily necessity. Traffic jams everywhere. Sweating all the time.

I immediately go into research mode, my instinctive response after a thirty-year career as a climate scientist. Thailand has three climatic zones: equatorial, tropical savannah, and tropical monsoon. I scan the data and authoritatively declare the climatological temperatures and humidity levels in all three zones to be, technically speaking, atrocious.

The data sparks a flashback to a scene from our honeymoon. I'm flat on my back, having collapsed in a dusty field of trampled grass. I open my eyes, squint through the glare, and make out three figures—Steve, a Thai mahout, and his elephant—all looking down at me with concern. (Actually, the elephant was rather nonchalant.) That was my last afternoon in the Thai heat. For the remainder of the trip, Steve and I spent the siesta hour in our air-conditioned hotel room, engaged in more suitable newlywed activities.

Steve and I have two choices—keep applying to schools in countries with more temperate climates and hope for the best or take the plunge and go to Thailand.

"We can keep trying," Steve says, "but we're not getting any younger, and these age limits aren't going away. Like the man said, 'When you come to a fork in the road, take it.'"

I shake my head, less at Yogi Berra's inanity than at the unfairness of the age restrictions. I compare the Thai academic calendar with the climatic data. If we sign up to teach the second semester, October through February, we can avoid the hottest months, March and April, and the subsequent rainy season. We'll have to cross our fingers and hope we don't end up in the equatorial zone, near the border with Malaysia, where a long-simmering and occasionally violent insurrection would add political sizzle to the heat.

"Okay," I say. "Let's do it." It isn't exactly the adventure I had imagined, but an adventure it will be.

"You're going to love Thailand. It truly is the Land of Smiles. The children will steal your hearts. I'm so happy for you two!" Kelsey's exuberance lifts our spirits. We pay the program fee and start making plans for an early October departure.

We make appointments for travel vaccinations. We book one-way flights to Chiang Mai, in northern Thailand, where we'll spend our first week at an orientation. That's when we'll get our teaching placement, which could be anywhere in the country.

We have plenty of time before we get on a plane in October. Plenty of time to wonder whether this adventure will turn out to be a misadventure. But we're determined to teach abroad, and, at our age, the world isn't exactly our oyster. Thailand is willing to take a chance on us, so we'll take a chance on Thailand.

The Teacher's Lesson

At the start of every term, I ask my ESOL students in Washington to name their biggest English challenges. The exercise is supposed to be reassuring to new immigrants in America. Knowing that others share their challenges and that we'll face them together in class should comfort them . . . or so I thought. Eleven weeks ago, my spring term level 3 class came up with this list, which I write again on the whiteboard:

<u>English Challenges</u>
- shopping (Larissa)
- doctor's appointments (Marlena)
- parent-teacher meetings (Naima)
- email (Federico)
- telephone calls (Keiko)
- asking directions (Ari)

"Do you remember this list from the first day of class?" I ask. Of course, they do. Their challenges haven't magically disappeared. "Today we'll discuss solutions. Talk with your partner for five minutes. How can you make these situations easier?"

The egg-timer rings, and together we create a parallel list of Solutions. Marlena, who has lived in Washington for decades speaking only Spanish, suggests that Larissa, a doctor and grandmother recently arrived from Russia, *take a shopping list*, in English, to the grocery store, so she can ask for help more easily.

Larissa, in turn, tells me to write *take a friend to the clinic* and, with a wink for Marlena, adds, "Better if your friend is a doctor."

Marlena's face lights up as she says, "I am agree!"

Classroom moments like these give me the warm fuzzies. Even if Marlena never learns that *agree* is a verb, her hours in ESOL class will have been time well spent. Larissa understands her perfectly.

"Naima, what solutions did you and Federico discuss for your parent-teacher meetings?" I ask.

"Pardon?" Naima replies, relying on her Moroccan French more than English.

To my chagrin, but predictably, Federico answers for her. "The problem is that the teacher of the son of Naima speaks too fast. I told Naima to ask the teacher to speak slowly." His English is heavily accented, but his rapid-fire speech is that of the lawyer he was in Venezuela. He dresses for class as if he were making closing arguments in court. I imagine he'll change out of his snappy suit and purple bow tie before his shift tonight washing dishes at the diner.

"Pardon?" Naima repeats.

Enunciating the words clearly, I add *ask people to speak slowly* to our list.

Sitting quietly, Ari has the perfect posture of a statue. With his orange robes, shaven head, horn-rimmed glasses, and beatific smile, he may as well be meditating as he waits patiently for Keiko to finish copying the list into her Hello Kitty notebook. I ask him, "What would *you* suggest for Naima when she meets with the teacher?"

The monk seems to consider the question but offers no answer, which makes me reconsider having asked it. What was I thinking? He is so young. How could he have any notion of a parent-teacher meeting in an American elementary school?

When we all introduced ourselves on the first day of class, Ari told us about his monastery on Sixteenth Street in northwest Washington. I've since learned that it is a Buddhist temple and that it follows the Theravada tradition.

I've been reading up on Thailand. Ninety-five percent of the population practices Theravada Buddhism. Maybe Ari is Thai. If so, could we arrange a language exchange—half an hour of English, half an hour of Thai? But wait, Thai monks can't be alone with a woman. We couldn't meet in the classroom. Maybe a café? Do monks drink coffee? Yikes, was I wrong to pair him with Keiko? Oh, it's all too complicated.

"When the mother meets the teacher, the teacher will be compassionate," says Ari deliberately, now having given sufficient thought to Naima's predicament. "The mother should not be afraid."

Naima's dark eyes, magnificent under her burgundy headscarf, smile gently as she absorbs her classmate's calm, clear advice. Is this Ari the teacher speaking? Does he welcome people to his temple for meditation class with compassion? And how should I summarize his suggestion on the whiteboard?

Ari's serenity intrigues me, appeals to me. It's even infectious when I observe him in class. I don't know why I find the idea of meeting with this man in orange robes to be such a challenge. And yet it's just like my reaction to my rabbi, to my friend who claims to be a shamanic healer, even to some yoga teachers. I like to keep conversation grounded and concrete. When it veers toward the spiritual, I veer away.

I add *don't be afraid, people are kind* to our Solutions list. It's supposed to be comforting. And I want to believe Ari is right. But are people kind if you can't speak their language and don't know how to respect their religion?

I could fill pages with my worries, but what would be the point? I need to stop fretting. I look at Ari's face, the antithesis of anxiety. Can I learn this from him? From Thailand?

Authentication in Progress

To teach in Thailand, the only credential an American needs is a college diploma. They take your word that you can teach English, but they want to see that diploma. And they want it authenticated.

Authentication involves a notary public, a state secretary of state (an office of which I've been oblivious until now), and the Thai Embassy. It's a process. It takes time.

If your diploma is in Latin, there's one more step: translation. We're waiting for a translation of Steve's diploma. Mine is in English, although in high school, I wanted one in Latin. Ivy League diplomas are in Latin.

Lux et Veritas, Yale's motto invoking light and truth, was inspiring, but when, as a high school senior, I visited the campus, its gray Gothic gloom wasn't. Instead, looking for a touch of grace, I went to Brown. *In Deo Speramus*. In God we hope.

I didn't find grace. Freshman year was a disaster. I know that "first-years" is the preferred term these days, but in 1977 we were all freshmen, regardless of gender identity. Saying "first-years" conjures images of Hogwarts, and my first year at college was anything but magical.

My classmates intimidated me. Some were supersophisticated private-school graduates who had already studied half the course material, all of which was new to me. Many got monthly allowances, while I scrubbed pots in the dining hall to qualify for financial aid. At night, missing her weekly sessions with her analyst, my roommate gave me an unsettling tutorial on alcohol abuse at her boarding school, the imperfect effectiveness of various contraceptives, and how to deal with the consequences. "Thanks for listening," she'd say, leaving me to fret about her troubles and my own in my narrow dormitory bed.

The campus film society was my escape. Sitting alone in the dark, the foreign films flickering in shades of gray, I decided I didn't belong at Brown.

So I transferred to UC Berkeley, sight unseen. Solo, I headed west with one suitcase, *California Dreamin'* on cassette tape, and hopes of a better fit.

Let There Be Light is embossed on my Berkeley diploma. And there was light.

My co-op housemates were the light of my Berkeley life. Telescope gazers, hacky sack players, conga drummers, pot growers. People in the closet and people coming out. Undocumented people and people who would never be able to go home again. Everyone was so different from me that comparison was pointless. A middle-class Jewish girl from Massachusetts who liked movies was just another sliver of color in a kaleidoscopic display. But I had more self-confidence as a sliver at Berkeley than I did as a shadow at Brown.

Did I need to transfer to overcome my freshman insecurities? Probably not. Did I find my authentic self in California? No, I'm still on that journey. But the vision of the world, and of my place in it, that I formed at Berkeley helped me find the path.

Now I'll pack another suitcase, stash my authenticated diploma under the zippered lining, and give the kaleidoscope another turn. Whatever Thailand reveals, I'll find my place in the pattern. I'll try not to fret over little frustrations. Steve will help me keep them in perspective. And when I need a break, there will be a movie theater where I'll find a little comfort for a few hours, not alone this time, but with a roommate who will hold my hand.

A Crash Course in Thai
at the Jersey Shore

I like learning foreign languages. As a child, I picked up the rudiments of Yiddish, the language my parents and grandparents used in conversations they deemed unsuitable for little ears. The Hebrew of the Bible and Jewish liturgy came easily at religious school, and writing the letters right to left was my earliest attempt at calligraphy. In high school, while the cool kids sang along with Carole King and Elton John, I was memorizing songs by Edith Piaf and Mercedes Sosa. The music helped me in my French and Spanish classes, and it gave me glimpses of cultures that, at the time, I had neither the opportunity nor the means to visit.

Over the years, for business and vacation travel, I've learned basic words of politesse (*hello, excuse me, please, thank you*) and survival (*where, left, right, how much, bathroom, no thank you*) in Russian, Arabic, and German, then promptly forgot them upon returning home. Lately, Italian classes are pure pleasure, especially when they're in Taormina or Rome, but *la bella lingua* isn't coming nearly as easily as its sister languages did decades ago, before the language acquisition regions of my brain started to shrivel.

Getting ready for Thailand, I'm worried. I'll need more than tourist Thai if I'm going to manage conversations with other teachers at school, a bank teller, or an ER doctor.

Steve is less concerned. "Plenty of Americans before us have survived in Thailand without a word of Thai," he reasons. But worried I remain.

Years ago my mother and I went to Switzerland, and the morning after our flight her legs were red and swollen. Fearing deep vein thrombosis, we went to the emergency room. The hospital experience was one of the highlights of Zurich—even more memorable than the Appenzeller cheese factory. The handsome young doctor treated Mom like royalty and, in impeccable English, assured her she would be fine. She was charmed, particularly when they told us there would be no charge for the visit. But I felt like the Ugly American, unable to speak Swiss German and dependent on the global dominance of the English language to get us through what might have been a real emergency. In a comparable situation in Thailand, we might not be so lucky.

"You're obsessing," Steve says, but he admits I have a point. Though he's not much of a language buff—he bid most of the German he learned in high school and college *auf Wiedersehen* long ago—he's willing to give Thai a try. We agree to spend the summer learning as much of the language as we can before we land in Chiang Mai in October.

Now we are in Steve's hometown at the Jersey shore to escape the swelter of a Washington summer and visit with friends and family. Other than teaching an English conversation class at the Atlantic City Free Public Library and swimming in the ocean, we have few demands on our time.

I begin hunting for a Thai language class, or maybe a private tutor, at the shore. The Internet and the yellow pages yield nothing, and the foreign language departments at local colleges are equally disappointing.

Mandy, the lifeguard at the beach who is an ESOL teacher during the school year, suggests a different approach—finding a class online.

"Trust me," she says, "this is the wave of the future. I understand your hesitation. Remote learning sounds so, well, remote. But wait and see. Soon people everywhere will be learning online, and not just for language lessons."

I'm dubious about talking to people through a computer screen, but I'll humor her. After all, Steve and I trust Mandy with our lives every morning as we swim side by side in an otherwise empty ocean. I check out the major international language schools. They offer Tagalog, Tamil, and Turkish online, but apparently not Thai. Not many months later, I will have to put my skepticism aside. The Covid-19 pandemic will make Mandy's prediction a reality, and a challenge, for teachers and students all around the globe, including me. But this summer at the shore, we won't be studying Thai remotely.

As a last resort, I look for recorded audio courses. Like the language schools, most of the big-name audio course companies offer dozens of languages, including some so obscure they are designated endangered, but not Thai. This should be a red flag, but, undaunted, I continue my search and finally stumble on the Pimsleur Method. The Thai course is no longer available to purchase, but our local library has an old version. I'll be able to renew my checkout every two weeks—no one puts a hold on the Thai course all summer.

We listen to the introduction and learn that, like Chinese, Thai is a tonal language. Actually, Thai has five tones, more than either Cantonese or Mandarin. We begin to understand why no one seems to teach, or want to learn, Thai. It's too dang hard!

I used Pimsleur to learn a little Italian before my first trip to Italy, and the Thai course is identical in methodology. We'll hear and repeat phrases and conversations that might be useful to a visitor, but instead of asking the pretty lady how to find Via Veneto in Rome, we'll ask her how to find Thanon Sukhumvit in Bangkok. Then we'll learn to ask her to join us for a drink. When we inquire if she's hungry and invite her for dinner, she, like the *signorina*, will politely decline.

Almost every day, Steve and I take turns with the lessons. He studies in the morning and accumulates a stack of notes on index cards. I work in the afternoon, when he's at the beach. I join him for a dip when the sun sinks in the sky and the temperature starts to drop.

After a few weeks, we start sprinkling tidbits of Thai into our conversations. *Hello. I'd like two bottles of beer, please. How much is the bill?*

As evening approaches, one of us will inquire about dinner. I ask the Thai way: *"Gin khao mai?"* Do you want to eat rice?

Steve, who has never much cared for rice, declines with the multipurpose *mai pen rai*. His punch line, "But I'd love a steak sub," gets a little stale after a few weeks.

We'll later learn that, while Thai people use *mai pen rai* to say "no, thanks," they also use it as an indirect "yes, please," avoiding appearing greedy while inviting a more insistent second offer.

Our audio course is all about listening and speaking, so we can't read or write any of these useful conversational morsels. I find an illustrated Thai alphabet chart. Are these ornate letters, all filigree and curlicues, really supposed to look like chickens, eggs, monkeys, monks, boats, and bells? I try, but the forty-four consonants and thirty-two vowels, not to mention the various tone markings, quickly overwhelm me.

"Don't sweat the alphabet," Steve says. He's convinced we

can manage as illiterates in Thailand. I'm convinced we should at least be able to read street signs and write our names.

"Once we're settled," I suggest, "we'll find a local teacher who can give us real lessons."

The look on Steve's face is enough to convey *mai pen rai*, which I'll choose to interpret as I please. This will be a conversation for another day.

Fostering Love

"Fear not, little Min," I say in a hush as I brush Minerva's black fur. "We'll take care of you." Her wide-open eyes, fixed on mine, say, "I'm not so sure." She stretches, steps across the sofa, and curls into Steve's lap. Minnie knows where to find the love.

Her entire life, Minerva has been quiet and serene, rarely a cause for worry. Until now. How will she survive our absence?

The rest of the family will be fine. We're concerned about my mother, but she's the healthiest ninety-five-year-old I know, and it is too morbid to consider postponing this adventure until she's no longer with us. When we broached the subject with her, she responded, *"Gey gezunt,"* Yiddish for "Go in good health." My traditional reply, *"zai gezunt,"* stay well, carried more emotion than ever before, but I have faith that she'll survive our absence.

So will our daughter Rose. She's an independent sort, working and going to grad school in New York. We'll keep in touch by email—by phone in an emergency. If she can swing it, she might visit during semester break.

Minerva is a different story. In theory, she's Rose's cat. In reality, Rose left her in our care after high school and has since developed an allergy to dander. When she recently took Minnie for a few weeks, her eyelids swelled up so much she couldn't see.

Steve, who has been taking allergy pills since we adopted Minerva thirteen years ago, has been fretting all summer. My husband is not generally a fretter—I do more than enough fretting for the two of us—but the idea of leaving Minnie with anything short of the perfect family has him seriously stressed. We've struck out with all of our cat-loving friends, relatives, and neighbors. Even the community message board, usually a font of solutions for any domestic problem, has come up dry.

Is this Steve's secret plan? Feign enthusiasm for an adventure teaching abroad, then use Minerva as an excuse to stay home, reading in his rocker, Minnie on his lap?

I'm not so easily deterred. My last hope is my book-club friend Tracy, whose daughter Zeenie (do all fourteen-year-old Maxines insist on nicknames?) has been begging for a cat. Tracy knows Minerva, who nestles on her shoes when I host meetings. Furry socks don't bother Tracy. Her house is full of critters—a dog, a guinea pig, and turtles.

Today Tracy and Zeenie are coming to the shore. I'm praying that Minnie and Zeenie hit it off, that Zeenie's eyelids don't puff up, and that another mouth to feed and litter box to clean won't overwhelm Tracy.

Tracy and Zeenie arrive with a dozen fresh eggs from their new backyard henhouse. Four different sizes and colors, from four different layers.

"How lovely," I say. But have those hens beaten Minerva to the family's last ounce of pet affection?

With visitors in the house, Minerva scoots upstairs. Zeenie, not so easily deterred, finds her in a patch of sunshine.

Over iced tea and blueberry cobbler at the kitchen table, Steve and I talk with Tracy. We play up Minnie's sweet disposition and tidy habits. We admit she's a picky eater, though we don't mention the salmon Steve grills for her dinners. As it happens, Zeenie is fussy, too. She eats only white foods. I make a last-minute menu switch. Instead of peach pie for dessert, we'll go for frozen custard. It's a Jersey shore boardwalk classic, and there is no food whiter than vanilla soft serve. We aim to please.

When Minerva pads downstairs, Zeenie is close behind. She declines the cobbler with its offensively blue berries, but she isn't hungry anyway. She's enthralled.

Zeenie speaks the magic words. "Can we take her? Please?"

Tracy regards Minerva, sprawled on a kitchen chair, then her daughter. "How could I say no to that sweet face? Or this one?"

I exhale my gratitude for Tracy, Zeenie, and all things bright and beautiful. Steve exhales his ambivalence.

Minnie stretches, jumps down, and rubs her flank against Zeenie's leg. She knows where to find the love.

Steve looks at Tracy, who is smiling as she looks at Zeenie, who is smiling as she strokes Minerva's head. Then he looks at me. I'm smiling, too. Under the table, I find his hand. He can't muster a smile yet. I squeeze his fingers, to remind him where to find the love.

Standing on Her Own Two Hands

"Did you catch Joyce's handstand today?" I ask my yoga teacher and mentor, Martha, as we settle in at our favorite restaurant for one last lunch before my departure. We both love the Ethiopian food and the location, right next door to the studio. And I love the painted mural over the bar with the long-limbed woman in silhouette striding purposefully through her earth-toned world. In it, I see Martha.

Martha is an angular, blonde Swiss German, and the curvy figure with the halo of dark hair in the mural is clearly from the Horn of Africa, but both women radiate the same message: "I know where I'm headed, I'm going to get there, and I'm going to savor every step of the journey." What must it be like to travel through life with such confidence, such a sense of joy?

"Yes, I saw that handstand." Martha doesn't miss much. "Good for Joyce!"

"First time without assistance," I say. It was a big moment for Joyce, whose downcast eyes and hunched shoulders usually telegraph the opposite of confidence. For as long as I've been Martha's apprentice, Joyce has been working on her handstands, doing what Martha calls "donkey work," planting two hands on the floor and kicking first one leg, then the other, up and down and up and down. Today, one leg went up, and then the other, before both came down from a brief but respectable handstand.

It was a big moment for me, too. Months ago, the first time Martha trusted me to assist students in handstands, Joyce tried to kick up, but with insufficient oomph. I tried to catch her leg, but with insufficient skill. Joyce's foot crashed into my face, fortunately with insufficient momentum to do serious damage. I learned a lesson in self-preservation from that episode, but all Joyce learned was one more reason to fear the pose. Today, she finally overcame that fear.

"Good for Joyce," Martha repeats. "But tell me all about your plans for Thailand. Where will you teach?"

"No concrete plans yet," I tell her, as I tell everyone who asks this question. "We have no idea where we'll be living. We won't know anything until we get there and they match us with a school. We might be teaching English to corporate types in Bangkok, or to school kids in the provinces, or to anybody anywhere."

All this uncertainty has been unsettling to some friends (and to me), but it doesn't faze Martha, who embraces the yogic principle of living in the present without wasting mental energy worrying about the future. She has an appetite for adventure. Whether it's standing on her hands, becoming a certified yoga teacher, or moving to another continent, Martha has done it. And she wants me to do it, too.

"And they'll also match you with a yoga studio, right?" Martha asks with a wink. "You *will* teach yoga in Thailand, of course."

As I always do when faced with Martha's perpetual positivity, I dial my own optimism up a notch.

"I sure would like to," I say. "But it doesn't look promising."

I've done some research. There's exactly one studio in

Thailand dedicated to the alignment-based yoga method of Indian guru B. K. S. Iyengar, the method Martha and I practice. It's in Bangkok, and the director is an American named Howard. His photo on the studio's website is a simple head shot—not a picture of him in some superadvanced, show-off pose. His hair is white, and his eyes reveal a gentle soul. I could see myself working for this man. But even if we end up in Bangkok, would he hire a newly minted yoga teacher who can't speak Thai?

"You know, Dian, teaching is a practice, just like asana," Martha says. "If you don't use it, you lose it."

She's right, of course. Though I've been teaching only a class or two per week, slowly honing the skills she's taught me, it's enough to know they need to be kept sharp. And enough to have felt that motivational zing when students make progress. Month by month, I see their bodies changing, sitting straighter and standing taller, and I get a little zing. It's the same little zing I get from my ESOL students whose progress never fails to impress and inspire me. And then there's Joyce and her handstand. Joyce overcoming her fear. That's a big zing.

"Do you remember when you asked me about apprenticeship?" Martha, now in full coaching mode, asks. But before she can begin her pep talk, lunch arrives. A huge brass platter topped with mounds of brick-red lentils, golden yellow cabbage with carrots, bright magenta beets, and dark green collards. I close my eyes and take a deep, almost yogic inhalation. Martha tears an injera pancake but waits for my answer before scooping up her first bite.

Of course I remember. It took me weeks to muster the courage to ask Martha to be my mentor, and I fully expected her to say no. She would enumerate all my physical limitations: bum knees, twingey lower back, general stiffness. If she wanted to invest time and energy in a new apprentice, wouldn't she rather work with someone younger and healthier, someone with more years of teaching ahead?

I should have known better. I was a challenge. Of course Martha would take me on.

"It'll be hard work, but if you put in the effort, so will I," she told me.

It *was* hard work. In my late fifties, after decades of sitting on my butt hunched over a computer, I was suddenly spending most of my waking hours either practicing on my mat at home, assisting Martha in her studio classes, studying with other aspiring teachers, or, eventually, teaching. Each step along the yearslong path was a physical and psychological struggle, and I can't say I took them confidently or joyfully. But each made me stronger.

"You said you weren't interested in teaching other people," Martha reminds me. "You said you just wanted to teach yourself, to keep up your practice when you went abroad."

True, but now my sights are set higher. Teaching suits my personality, and teaching Iyengar yoga suits me to a T.

Iyengar yoga is famous for its focus on precise body alignment, which teachers coax out of students with a steady stream of imperatives. *Align your feet parallel to the sides of your mat. Press your feet into the floor. Straighten your knees.* And that's just scraping the surface of the dozens of instructions we give for mountain pose, which is basically standing on two feet. If practicing Iyengar yoga is for people who like structure, clarity, and order, then teaching Iyengar yoga is for people who like to *give* orders.

Steve was my first student, and I gave him plenty of orders. He laughed when he told me, "You need to recruit some other guinea pigs . . . for the sake of our marriage." But he meant it.

After just two sessions, he called it quits. I've since learned how to better temper correction with encouragement, but not before scaring off several would-be students who anticipated a relaxing session of deep breathing, not an hour of postural directives.

"But now you teach," Martha says, "and you can't quit. If you can't find a studio, look for a gym, or teach your English students yoga. Or teach Steve."

Martha's jokes never fail to make me laugh. I'm going to miss her. This yoga path she has helped me navigate could reach its end in Thailand. But maybe the image of Joyce standing on her hands will keep me moving forward, with intention, like that lady in the mural. Even if I don't know where I'm going.

Pack Up Your Troubles

US foreign policy often mystifies me, but I still trust that US Foreign Service officers are helping Americans abroad stay safe. That's why I've signed up for the State Department's traveler alerts. The day before our departure, their first message arrives in my inbox.

> *Health Alert: U.S. Embassy Bangkok, Thailand–*
> *October 2, 2019*
>
> *Event: Dengue is endemic throughout Southeast Asia, including Thailand, and is a leading cause of febrile illness among travelers . . . . Peak transmission occurs during warmer and wetter months, usually from May to October. The U.S. Consulate General in Chiang Mai has decided to limit outdoor evening events . . . due to several confirmed cases . . . .*

Dengue fever? As if hepatitis, influenza, Japanese encephalitis, typhoid, and tetanus weren't enough to worry about. We've just been vaccinated against all these. Our arms are still too sore to lift the packed and zipped suitcases waiting by the front door. To make matters worse, a travel guide someone gave me last week recommends the rabies vaccine as a precaution against the feral dogs roaming the streets of Thailand. But now there isn't time for the four injections in the rabies series. And there isn't time for a dengue vaccine, either.

"Fever, nausea, vomiting, aches and pain," I read to Steve. "And wait, it gets worse. Severe dengue: bleeding from the nose or gums, vomiting blood, blood in the stool…" My heart rate is climbing and I'm starting to sweat.

"Enough," Steve says, knowing how anxiety-inducing this symptom list is, and what a mosquito magnet I am. "You packed DEET, didn't you?"

With no idea how far we will be from a pharmacy or clinic, I packed every imaginable painkiller, first-aid supply, and prescription drug we could possibly need, including the insect repellent N,N-diethyl-meta-toluamide (DEET). Along with toothpaste, soap, sunscreen, air pollution masks, nail clippers, makeup, granola bars, and, in case Thai sweets aren't sweet enough for Steve, candy, it's enough to fill one of our two large suitcases. The other case has clothes, shoes, books, swim goggles, and my yoga mat. We'll take our computers and important documents in our carry-ons.

"Don't worry. We'll use the DEET until the rainy season is over, then we'll be fine," Steve says.

"The alert is from Chiang Mai! That's exactly where we're going first!" I know Steve knows full well where we're going. I'm just looking for a little acknowledgment of the danger we're facing.

"We'll be stuck indoors all week for orientation. We probably won't even have time to go outside and mingle with the mosquitos," he says reassuringly. "Don't worry. Relax. *Mai pen rai.*"

My eyebrows approach my hairline. (I have a very short forehead.) "You've been studying. I'm impressed!" I wouldn't have expected Steve to go as "all in" as he has—plodding through the language course, reading up on Thai history and culture, even checking the *Bangkok Post* website for daily news.

I've been studying too, reading every novel and memoir I can find that takes place in Thailand. The pickings are slim, but my favorite so far is Carole Hollinger's 1965 memoir *Mai Pen Rai Means Never Mind*. Her husband worked at the American Embassy in Bangkok, the very source of my current anxiety, and she is my role model. I imagine myself in her shoes, teaching English at Chulalongkorn University, making Thai friends, and adopting their *mai pen rai* approach to life. She was already more easygoing than I will ever be, but maybe I can take a page from her funny, mid-twentieth-century playbook and learn to stay cool and not sweat the small stuff.

Mai pen rai. Little do we realize how often we'll repeat those three little words during our time in Thailand. But we're not there yet. And before I get on that plane tomorrow, I'm going shopping. No harm in packing a second bottle of DEET in my carry-on, just in case that medical bag we call a suitcase doesn't make it to Chiang Mai. And maybe I need to stop reading the embassy alerts.

Wake Up and Smell
the Thai Coffee

Our first morning in Chiang Mai, Steve and I are up early and eager to explore, excitement negating the twelve-time-zone jet lag. But the moment we step outside our hotel, two quintessential features of Thai cities—heat and traffic—smack us back indoors. All we can see of the sidewalk-less street through the instant fog on our glasses is a swarm of swerving scooters. Many carry entire families—children sandwiched between parents, toddlers standing upright, women in slim skirts riding sidesaddle.

"We need to walk single file, close to the buildings. And close to each other, so one can pull the other out of harm's way," I tell Steve, whose sigh is as much agreement as I'm going to get. The desk clerk with the dazzling smile (another quintessential feature of Thailand) tells us not to worry—we'll find coffee within a few blocks.

We do. The Akha Ama coffeehouse is a welcome refuge. The café's industrial-chic decor and top-of-the-line espresso machines seem more Seattle than northern Thailand, as do the two English-speaking men in Lycra claiming the table next to us with their bicycle helmets. The only signs that we're in Thailand are the lotus flowers drawn in our cappuccinos' velvety foam, but Steve and I aren't complaining. We chose this spot over the outdoor coffee and smoothie carts for its air conditioning, not authenticity.

"Can you actually bike around Chiang Mai?" Steve asks the cyclists. The suggestion is suicidal, and I'll assume it's simply a polite conversation starter.

"Downtown is tough. But cycling the national park trail to Doi Suthep at dawn is awesome!" says the older man. "Damien and I do it every Sunday. Then we come here." Roy introduces himself and his bike buddy Damien. I pull my water bottle out of our backpack, and Roy grabs my arm.

"That's not tap wooder, is it?" he demands, his accent, stronger than Steve's, screaming his South Jersey roots. Once he's certain that we understand the necessity of bottled water, even for brushing our teeth, Roy shifts into high gear. He adores Chiang Mai, northern Thailand's largest city, with its open-air markets, nearby mountains for biking and hiking, and abundance of expats to show you the ropes. We listen and savor the excellent espresso. It's smooth, dark, and potent, the cup rimmed with toast-brown crema, the flavor heightened by the aroma of freshly roasted beans that fills the café.

Damien opens a paper bag and pulls out a crusty croissant and a perfect *pain au chocolat*. He sees my eyes widen and says, "Nearby is the best baker in Chiang Mai. From Belgium. Like me."

"And are you here in Thailand for the biking, or just for the pastries?" I ask Damien.

"Both. And the coffee. Most days, I work here at this café. The best coffee in Thailand."

"You came to Thailand from Belgium to be a barista?"

"No," he laughs, "I'm a programmer. I spend a few months a year here, then I move on. You know, a digital nomad." I *don't* know the term, but looking around the café I see other members of Damien's tribe—mostly Westerners, sitting alone, staring at screens, coffee cups on their tables as receipts for their "office" rent.

"How did you find Akha Ama?" Roy asks.

"Pure luck," I say. "We just arrived yesterday from the States. We're staying nearby, and we needed caffeine."

"No joke. This really *is* the best café in Thailand. Plus, the owner is Akha—that's one of the hill tribes in northern Thailand—and he sources the coffee there. Supports the community." I make a mental note. We'll be in Chiang Mai for a week, longer if we get jobs in the city. With a backstory like that, and coffee this good, we could become regulars here.

"So, what brings you to Thailand?" Roy asks.

"We're here to teach English," Steve tells Roy.

"Ah, English teachers. You'll be in good company. There must be a thousand here in Chiang Mai alone. A thousand times as many around the country."

Steve smiles at the thought of a vibrant expat community. I'm concerned we'll have lots of competition for jobs.

"Be careful—you don't want to end up hanging out with expat *farangs* in Thailand," chuckles Damien. "Or do you?"

Good question. Steve and I might have different answers. Whether Roy's statistics are accurate or not, I hadn't envisioned keeping company with English teachers, Lycra-clad expat retirees, or *farang* digital nomads. I am in Thailand to teach and get to know Thai people.

I catch Steve's eye. "Need more caffeine?"

The barista smiles broadly as he hands me two cups and asks, "You English teacher? I heard you talking to Roy." He says his name is Trek, and I leap at my first opportunity to introduce myself, in Thai, to a real person rather than to the recorded audio course instructor I've been talking to for months. I manage to tell him we are from America and that we are teachers, though he obviously already picked up those details. With the caffeine kicking in, the memorized snippets of dialogue roll off my tongue with a most self-satisfying fluency.

"Khru Dian," says Trek, using the Thai title for teacher, a sign of respect for the profession, "you speak Thai language!"

I laugh, genuinely amused, but also excited to reply with my favorite word from the audio course, "*Nidnoy*—just a little."

Trek seems to appreciate my attempt and to have overheard our entire conversation with the cyclists. "You want visit Thai hill tribes? I take you tomorrow, to Akha, in Chiang Rai, in my car. Can."

I take Trek's phone number and promise to think about it. The promise is more to myself than to Trek, and what I'll think about is the absurdity of the idea of venturing to remote regions of another province—where exactly is Chiang Rai, anyway?—with a perfect stranger. I may be seeking adventure, but I'm not ready for Thai highways. Though Trek makes an excellent cappuccino, and we'll probably see him again at the café, he won't be driving us to the hinterlands.

But we don't need to travel any farther to begin our adventure. We just need to step outside the café door. We are wide awake and ready to begin.

23andWe

Fortified by caffeine and our coffee-shop conversations, I'm a more confident pedestrian as we retrace our steps from Akha Ama to the hotel. The sign taped to the glass-walled meeting room reads *Teach the World Travel Orientation 0800 to 1700 Monday to Friday.* Yet it somehow feels like the start of someone else's adventure, not ours. Like when we dropped our daughter off at college.

Luggage lines the walls. Lots of young flesh is exposed, much of it tattooed. There's a buzz of anticipation in the chatter. People ask versions of the same questions: "Are you with Teach the World? When did you arrive? Where are you from? First time in Thailand? Is there any coffee?" Everyone seems to need reassurance that they are in the right place and have made the right decision.

But this isn't a college dorm, and there are no other parents. It is the breakfast room in a budget hotel in Chiang Mai. Mark, program director for Teach the World Travel and our lead trainer, is here to tell us everything we need to know to succeed as English teachers in Thailand.

First, though, comes a round-the-room session of twenty-five self-introductions. I take notes, so I'll have some chance of learning names. These young people's backstories could inspire several seasons of a late-Millennial reality TV series. A few have teaching experience, but most are in Thailand to put distance between themselves and troubles at home.

Monday morning's theme is the importance of understanding, respecting, and trying to adapt to Thai culture. Mark summarizes his key survival tips for *farang* teachers in Thailand.

Do: Smile. Learn how, when, and whom to *wai*. Dress conservatively. Bring food to school for your colleagues. Keep your cool. And smile.

Don't: Hold hands, hug, or kiss in public. Criticize the monarchy. Point your toes at people. Touch a monk. Suggest ways to improve anything. And please, if you want to return home alive, don't ride on scooters.

Recounting the story of the Canadian teacher whose first scooter ride marked his last day in Chiang Mai, and on Earth, Mark chokes up a bit. Emmaline, a recent college graduate from California whose brother was killed by a drunk driver, is a puddle of tears. Courtney, whose father is abusive, has a consoling arm around Emmaline.

Mark already told us that Thailand's per capita death rate due to traffic accidents is among the world's highest, which squares with conditions this morning on the streets of Chiang Mai. I'm not surprised that a foreign teacher contributed to the grim statistics.

But my eyes turn misty when Mark says, "The hardest thing I've ever had to do in this job was meet his parents at the airport and take them to the crash site. I tried to dissuade them, but they insisted." It's so easy to imagine Steve and me in the back seat of Mark's car, having flown—numb or hysterical or medicated—halfway around the globe, devastated by the loss of a child. A child we would have hoped would always remember to wear her helmet.

Over coffee break, the twenty-three twentysomethings are busy making sightseeing plans for our free afternoon later in the week. My initial impression of them as little lost lambs flies out the window—they've clearly done their research. The Canadians, Harlen (alcoholic mother), Hope (friend murdered by a home intruder), and Cody (recently homeless, currently nearly broke), are going hiking near Wat Phratat Doi Suthep, the gleaming Buddhist temple on the hillside. Cody wants to meditate with the monks at the *wat*, Hope feels claustrophobic in Chiang Mai and needs green space, and Harlen is going along for the company.

Billie (a runaway from the Midwest) has convinced a couple of other American girls to have their pictures taken with tigers. James, who recently came out to his evangelical family in Kentucky and now needs to be far away from them, disapproves of the tiger photo shoot, citing animal welfare concerns. Would Billie consider a visit to the elephant reserve, a rehab center for old, abused, and injured animals, instead?

Jordyn will go with Carly and Nicky to the Chiang Mai markets. Jennie and Benjy, from Australia, know a place in the outskirts of Chiang Mai with great *khao soi*, the northern Thai coconut curry with a double dose of noodles.

Like puppies, these young people are eager to bond and to explore their new world. That world includes Steve and me. Despite the relative lack of drama in our backstories, we seem to intrigue them. In every conversation, someone remarks about not being able to imagine their parents, or grandparents, uprooting their lives to teach in Thailand. In private, Steve and I refer to the group as the 23andWe, because we are not just a different generation; we feel almost a genetically different species.

Several groups invite us to join their outings. Whether they want to get to know us or simply need a parental figure in their life far from home, I find their warmth heartening and their energy infectious.

A bowl of noodles sounds good. How are the Australians planning to get to the restaurant?

"We found a place to rent scooters. Really cheap," says Jennie gleefully.

Steve smiles and manages to keep his eyeballs from rolling heavenward. I go in search of James, to arrange an excursion more suitable to our generation—an encounter with the elderly elephants.

Placement Prep

"Please be as open-minded as possible in filling out your placement preference form," Mark instructs us as we move one step closer to learning where we will be teaching.

Fortysomething Mark is midway in age between us and the 23andWe bunch, and he relates easily to everyone. Steve and I find his lessons on Thai history, government, and culture wonderfully engaging, but most of our classmates are doodling, daydreaming, or debilitated by jet lag. Though our days are filled with Mark's lectures, language lessons with one of the Thai staff, and practical arrangements—opening bank accounts, getting mobile phones, enrolling in insurance plans—the main focus of orientation week is placing each would-be English teacher in a suitable Thai school.

Despite Mark's admonition not to be picky, most of us have clear notions of our ideal placement. Some envision gorgeous tropical beaches and want to be near the Gulf of Thailand or the Andaman Sea. For others, the city lights of Bangkok beckon.

Steve and I want placements in the same town. We'd be even happier to share a single position, if that's possible. We check the boxes to indicate our preference for adult students (like we teach at home) or high school, in northern Thailand (for its marginally cooler climate), with housing options within walking distance (because we aren't getting a scooter).

We debate Bangkok. About a third of our group will end up in the capital, which is far and away Thailand's largest metropolis. Steve thinks we'd do well in an international city—a feature of Washington that we love—and reminds me about the yoga studio in Bangkok. I remind him of the heat, traffic, and air pollution we encountered there twenty-nine years ago. We compromise—meaning I get my way. We leave the Bangkok box blank, but we'll consider a job there if we get an offer.

Mark pulls us aside and tells us, "We're making a special effort for you two. Placing couples can be a challenge." He hesitates before spelling out our real problem. "The bigger issue, frankly, is your age. Thai schools tend to prefer younger teachers. But, fear not. I'm sure we'll find something suitable."

This hits us like an icy water balloon, which we've just learned is a key element of Songkran, the Thai New Year celebration in April. The only reason we are here in Thailand is that our age ruled out all our other choices and we were told it *wouldn't* be a problem here.

After a night of agita, Mark comes through with a placement possibility. A high school in Tak, near the Myanmar border, will hire me as a full-time English teacher while Steve would teach "Teen Health" once a week after school.

It's far from perfect, but at least it's an offer. Figuring we might renegotiate the lopsided teaching load, we spend the evening doing research. Tak is known for its vast expanses of undeveloped terrain, a hydroelectric dam, and a drug-resistant strain of malaria. Travel from Tak to anywhere else in Thailand requires a long ride over rough mountain roads. Teen Health is code for sex ed. We can't imagine the syllabus, which must somehow square Thailand's (or maybe just Bangkok's) famed openness about sexuality with its conservative views on public displays of affection, or what English vocabulary Steve would need to teach before presenting the course material.

The next morning we thank Mark but tell him that, unless we can rebalance the teaching load, we'll pass on Tak.

Mark nods. "Fear not," he says again. "I'm sure we'll find something suitable."

Our eyes light up the following morning when Mark asks, "Can you do a video interview after lunch? A school in central Thailand is offering a shared teaching position." He tells us that it's a private Montessori school in Pathum Thani province, about an hour's drive from Bangkok.

Steve puts on a button-down shirt and tie. I brush my hair and apply a little makeup, which I'm sure to sweat away within an hour. Mark tells us the interview with the school director, Dr. Pat, is a formality—the position is ours if we want it.

Dr. Pat's face on our laptop screen is smiling. She asks us about our trip from America, our impressions of Thailand, our family. She is stylish, charming, and flattering. "Your résumés are impressive. And you speak English so clearly! I have always wanted American teachers for our English-immersion program." Then, her smartphone in hand, she takes us on a virtual tour of the Pathum Thani Prep campus.

There is a pretty garden with flowers and fountains at the school entrance and a beautiful swimming pool, which, she assures us, we would be welcome to use. We can't make out the apartment building, across a small alley, where Dr. Pat says we could live almost rent-free. The final stop is the classroom. It is modern, well equipped, and clearly designed for very young children.

"What grade level is this class?" Steve asks.

"Kindergarten. K1 and K2. Eleven children in all, though

we expect a few more to enroll. You will love them." After showing us the playground, complete with a colorful jungle gym and a miniature running track, Dr. Pat asks, "Can you come on Monday?"

"It's a lovely school," Steve tells Mark after the interview. "The director was gracious and enthusiastic. The job-sharing arrangement is just what we wanted. The housing situation seems great—no need to deal with traffic."

"It's kindergarten," Mark reminds us, "and Thai kids start K1 at age two and a half." He wants to know, "Will you be okay with that?"

It's not exactly what we had in mind, but it's far better than spending our time in Thailand hunkered down in Tak, Steve having next to nothing to do at school, in a town offering next to nothing by way of other activities, located near next to nothing.

Steve and I exchange a look. "We'll be okay," we answer in unison.

That remains to be seen. We won't be teaching adults or high schoolers as we had hoped, and we won't be in the slightly cooler north of the country, but at least we'll be teaching in Thailand. Prepared or not, we are going to Pathum Thani Prep.

Welcome to Pathum Thani.
Any Questions?

At noon on Monday, just as Mark promised, Khun Chailai is waiting for us. In her canary yellow sheath dress and matching handbag and stilettos, she's easy to find in the gray-and-beige arrivals lounge of Don Muang International Airport in the outskirts of Bangkok, close to Pathum Thani province.

Khun Chailai is our agent. Whether she represents Teach the World Travel, Pathum Thani Prep, us, or her own interests is unclear. It will remain unclear for our entire stay in Thailand, but today it's enough to know that she speaks English and will show us the way to school. During the half-hour drive, she explains her job with a chuckle: "I am your personal paperwork lady." Though we will live and work in Pathum Thani, Khun Chailai's office in Bangkok will handle our contracts, work permits, visas, and paychecks.

Actually, we won't get paychecks. "The last workday of each month, I send a messenger with your salary, in cash," she explains. Steve and I exchange glances. This doesn't sound kosher, but our half-day ordeal opening a bank account last week in Chiang Mai convinced us that cash transactions might be the simplest way to manage finances in Thailand. We don't ask questions.

We turn off the highway into a small alley, a *soi*, and stop in front of a two-story stucco building with Thai lettering over the entrance. The first letter might be shaped like a fish, *pla*, one of the few animal words I know. During our big kitchen cleanup last month before leaving Washington, I found a bottle of Thai fish sauce, *nam pla*, purchased for some long-forgotten recipe. Its fermented, vinegary taste had made Steve gag, but it seemed to have an infinite shelf life and for years I couldn't part with it. If nothing else comes of this adventure in Thailand, our tidy pantry will have been worth the trouble.

Or maybe it's not a fish, and the sign doesn't say Pathum Thani Prep. It doesn't matter—Khun Chailai announces, "Here we are!"

Opening the door of Khun Chailai's air-conditioned minivan, we are greeted by a blast of hot air and three smiling women who escort us indoors. I'm smiling, too, and trying to figure out who these people are and when we'll meet Dr. Pat. We're taken to her office, but where is the elegant, enthusiastic school director who interviewed us last week?

Across the conference table, Khru Nok is smartly dressed in a slim skirt and cropped silk jacket. She is truly stunning, and it's hard to take my eyes off her perfectly symmetrical features, flawless complexion, and brilliant smile. She has some sort of administrative role at the school, though her title, *khru*, means she is also a teacher. "Sign, please, and write the date," she asks politely, signaling a stack of documents, all in Thai.

"Are these our contracts?" Steve asks. Though he never practiced professionally, he has a law degree and doesn't sign papers willy-nilly.

"Teaching contract, housing agreement, and some government forms," Khru Nok replies. Khun Chailai assures us they are all legit, checks that our signatures match the ones in our passports, then crosses out the dates we've written and changes

2019 to 2562.

"In Thailand, we count the years from the Buddha's birth, especially for official documents," she explains. Though it took a week, our bodies have adjusted to the twelve-hour time difference between DC and Bangkok. I wonder how long it will take our minds to adjust to the Buddhist Era.

As if she could hear my thoughts, Khru Nok smiles and assures me, "*Mai pen rai.* No problem. We use the *farang* calendar at Prep."

The oldest woman, an apron covering her baggy T-shirt and indigo waders, jingles her key chain and says something in Thai that causes Khru Nok to announce, "The General is arriving."

The General? Is this how the staff refers to Dr. Pat? I glance out the office window but see no one on the lawn or the *soi*. Across the *soi* is a two-story building that vaguely resembles a mid-twentieth-century Southern California roadside motel. Is this the teachers' housing, for which we just signed a rental agreement, sight unseen? Is the woman with the keys—is her name really Pee Wee?—the caretaker?

This time it's Teacher Miranda who seems to read my mind. "The General has invited you to lunch, and I will join you. But first Pee Wee will show you your apartment." Teacher Miranda has an open, friendly face with laugh lines at the corners of her eyes and deep dimples. She speaks English better than the others. Her accent isn't Thai, but it's not one I recognize.

Before we leave, Khru Nok has one more request. "I will order your teacher shirts this afternoon. What size, please?" By American standards, Steve and I are both decidedly medium, but assuming Thai sizes are scaled to Thai bodies, we both guess large and follow Khun Chailai to her minivan.

"Good luck," she chirps, as we take our bags. "Text me if you have any problems."

"Thanks," I say, "for everything." What I don't know is that this will be the last we see of Khun Chailai, who will deal with us strictly through Khru Nok in the months ahead.

Pee Wee insists on wheeling our two huge suitcases across the *soi* and lugging them upstairs. Halfway down the exterior corridor, she stops at a wooden door with the number three painted in white. She pulls a paper clip with two identical keys attached out of her apron pocket and demonstrates how to unlock the padlock. She then goes through an elaborate pantomime to warn us never to lock the doorknob lock and hands Steve the keys.

"No key for the doorknob?" Steve asks.

"*Mai mee* key *kha*." Pee Wee's response is disappointing from a security perspective, but I'm pleased to have at least understood her message. We'd better not lock the doorknob; she doesn't have a key.

Pee Wee, Teacher Miranda, and Khru Nok stand back to let Steve and me cross the threshold first. The walls of the living room are pristine with a fresh coat of off-white paint. Shiny sheets of plastic, printed with a woodgrain pattern and Scotch-taped at the seams, cover the concrete floors. My first breath of off-gassing chemicals tells me the IKEA-style furniture is brand new. The bedroom sports a new mattress on the double bed and, most thrillingly, a wall-mounted, remote-controlled AC unit. The kitchen is outfitted with a small stainless steel sink, a toaster in an unopened box, and a chest-high refrigerator, perfectly clean and perfectly empty.

The back door opens onto a tiny terrace with a single-tap sink and a second door. Steve opens it to find, literally, a water closet—a semienclosed space, the size of a phone booth, which clearly wasn't included in the recent remodel. We both peer in to discover a showerhead attached to a wall-mounted water heater, a urinal, and a toilet. Instead of toilet paper, which would be impossible to keep dry, we have the quintessentially Thai bum gun, whose value, we will soon discover, is not limited to personal hygiene. The bum gun—a hose with an attached spray head that serves as a handheld bidet—will be ideal for washing away the trails of tiny ants crisscrossing the walls and for excavating the cracks in the well-worn tiles that seem to be their points of entry.

Back in the kitchen, Pee Wee asks nervously, "Okay *mai kha?*"

"Oh, yes, very nice," I answer, suppressing thoughts of volatile organic compounds, the bathroom, and the lack of AC in the kitchen and living room.

Steve is, as usual, more sensitive. "Beautiful," he says enthusiastically. "I'm sure we'll be very happy here. Thank you. Really, it's beautiful."

"Bea-u-ti-ful, *kha!*" repeats Pee Wee, smiling to herself as she guides us back down to the *soi,* where she offers a deep *wai* to a man with a cane waiting by a pickup truck.

After offering her own *wai,* Teacher Miranda says, "General, please meet Teacher Steve and Teacher Dian."

"Welcome, welcome!" he says and, with a very un-Thai gesture, reaches to shake our hands. "Dr. Pat is sorry she is not here today. She is at another school, so she sent me to welcome you." He is tall by any standard, and his stooped shoulders, round tummy, and broad face give the impression of a gentle, giant panda. With an appealing twinkle in his droopy eyes, he adds, "And I always follow the boss's orders."

He introduces himself as Aphakorn, but Teacher Miranda continues to address him as "General" all afternoon. No one explains his role at school, and all I can imagine is the General, sitting on a folding chair, thumping his cane on the ground while Thai children march around a schoolyard in some sort of junior ROTC program.

"Teacher Steve," he says, "you sit beside me, please. Ride shotgun, yes?" With a little bow, he opens the back door for Teacher Miranda and me and checks that we all fasten our seatbelts. Wincing, he lifts his large frame into the driver's seat and announces, "We go for lunch!"

The General enjoys driving and pointing out the sights of Pathum Thani. He speaks slowly, unsure of his English, as he identifies a half dozen government buildings with steep red-tiled roofs and stucco walls adorned by enormous gold-framed portraits of the king and the Thai national emblem, the golden half-man half-eagle Garuda. The General focuses our attention on the police station and immigration office and gently suggests we be diligent about fulfilling all our visa obligations.

"You know the area well," I say, preferring to leave bureaucratic issues to our personal paperwork lady and curious to decipher this man in baggy jeans whom everyone treats with such respect.

"My family has been here a long time," the General replies. It will be months before we learn more of the family's position in Pathum Thani.

Teacher Miranda hasn't uttered more than a few words since we met. I turn to her and ask, "And how long have *you* been in Pathum Thani?"

"It will be eight years next July," she replies after a moment's calculation.

The General chimes in with, "Teacher Miranda is a senior member of our contingent from the Philippines."

Is this petite, sweet-faced woman an officer in the military training program? And why are these two our welcoming committee? Seeing my confusion, Teacher Miranda explains, "There are many teachers from the Philippines at school. We work mostly with the younger grades."

"Oh. I see," I say. "And what grade do you teach?"

"Kindergarten. The English-immersion Montessori program. I'm the head teacher," she replies.

Oh. *Now* I see. During our interview last week, it didn't occur to Steve or me to ask Dr. Pat if we'd be reporting to anyone other than her. And apparently it didn't occur to Dr. Pat to tell us that Teacher Miranda would be our boss.

When we arrive at the restaurant, the General knows exactly where he wants to sit, and the staff is happy to accommodate. He orders for the table, enough food for twice our number. Over lunch he asks Steve and me polite questions about our pre-teaching lives. He has clearly seen and studied our résumés. Teacher Miranda clearly has not. She doesn't say much during the meal, though she does answer Steve's question about who is teaching the class today.

"Teacher Candace," she says. "You'll meet her tomorrow morning." And so we learn that the eleven kindergarteners at Pathum Thani Prep already have two teachers. How does Teacher Miranda feel about having two new helpers in her classroom, or about the fact that they are us?

Teacher Miranda doesn't offer answers to my unspoken questions. Instead, she politely inquires, "General, how is Dr. Pat?"

"Fine, fine," the General responds. "She'll get a full report of our day together when she returns next week. Boss's orders!"

"When I marry, I hope my husband follows orders half as well," Teacher Miranda laughs, this time answering more of my unasked questions. The General and Dr. Pat are married. And

Miranda is not.

We leave the restaurant with a shopping bag full of leftovers, which the General insists we take to stock our empty fridge. Then he announces, "Next stop, Lotus!"

It's only midafternoon, but I'm exhausted. We left our hotel in Chiang Mai early in the morning, and our day has been one guessing game after another. I don't have the energy to ask what Lotus is, but we learn soon enough. The General parks the pickup at what may be most easily described as a Thai version of Walmart.

"Go with Teacher Miranda," he says. "Shop for your apartment. I will wait outside." Steve protests that the restaurant food will be plenty for several days, but the General's offer, though gentle and generous, is an order.

We don't know where to start. Food, a fan, cleaning supplies? Since Steve and I have not adopted (and during our entire stay in Thailand will not adopt) the Thai habit of starting the day with what we consider dinner food, we focus on *farang* breakfast items—cereal, milk, coffee, and fruit. Miranda helpfully explains the half dozen varieties of bananas and recommends a bunch that looks like a child-sized baseball glove, with short, fat, finger-length fruits, which she assures us are the sweetest we'll ever try. The bananas might be heavenly, but Steve's sweet tooth is legendary, and he adds a few candy bars to the cart just to be safe.

At the checkout, the General is waiting for us, insisting on paying the bill. But there's a problem—something about the mangoes. The General waves his hand and says to the cashier, *"Mai pen rai,"* and a lot of other things I don't understand. The upshot is that the mangoes don't make it into our shopping bag. I don't ask questions—bananas will suffice.

Before dropping us at our apartment, the General gives us

his phone number and makes us promise to call him—anytime, day or night—if we need anything.

"I am always on duty," he assures us.

We climb the stairs with our bundles. Steve finds the keys, unlocks the padlock, turns the doorknob, and moans, "Locked."

After a few minutes of jiggling the knob and fruitless speculation about who left the apartment last, we consider whether to call the General. Neither of us is eager to admit our stupidity or to summon him to our rescue. What could he do anyway? There's no key to the lock.

Working our way down the second-floor balcony, we knock on the other apartment doors. No one is home. It's late afternoon and the teachers must still be at school. We're really just wasting time, because they wouldn't have keys either. At the last empty apartment, I peer over the balcony at the *soi* and hear the swish of a broom. It's Pee Wee, sweeping leaves from the pavement.

She's our only hope, and we agree to face her together. We *wai* and then pantomime our predicament. It's not at all clear whether she understands us, but she answers in Thai and leads us back upstairs. She opens another apartment door, apparently her own, and comes out with a credit card, which she slides between the door and the jamb. With a click the lock is open.

This is the first but it won't be the last time Pee Wee comes to our rescue. Steve offers her a Snickers bar from our grocery bag, shows her his own credit card, and assures her we won't bother her again this evening.

Once inside, we heed Miranda's warning about the local ants, stash all the food, including the granola, in the fridge, and unpack our suitcases. At 8 p.m., with finally a chance to relax, we hear a knock at the door. It's Pee Wee.

She has two packages for us, one from Khru Nok and one

from the General. This is all we understand, though she says much more before finally asking, "Okay *mai kha*?"

This time, we are both enthusiastic in our thanks. "*Khop khun kha*," I say, and Steve chimes in "*Khop khun khrap*," before we bid her good night.

Steve opens the paper bag and pulls out three heavy mangoes with a sweet, flowery fragrance.

"I don't get it," I say. "What was the problem with the mangoes at the store?"

"Who knows," Steve says. "Maybe those weren't ripe? Maybe these come from the General's garden? Just consider it one of the mysteries of Pathum Thani. And don't ask questions."

This is a big ask. I *always* ask questions. I'm not a nosy person, but as a research scientist for thirty years, it was my job to ask questions. I'm much happier when I understand the basic workings of my world. Living in a place as enigmatic as Pathum Thani is going to take some adjustment. Maybe this is the challenge of my adventure in Thailand—to let mysteries remain mysteries, or at least to let understanding come in its own time.

But as I open Khru Nok's package, I have two more questions. "Could they be any bigger? Could they be any more orange?"

Between Steve's red hair and my blotchy pink skin, neither of us owns a stitch of orange clothing. But this morning we signed a contract. Somewhere in the fine print, did we agree to wear these enormous, crossing-guard-orange polo shirts, emblazoned with the Prep insignia, every day for the next five months?

Any other questions?

The Three-Day Rule

All we are saying (over and over again) is give Prep a chance.

"The first few days are never easy," Mark told our Chiang Mai orientation group before explaining Teach the World Travel's three-day rule. He assured us that if things don't work out, the program will find teachers a different placement, but not until we've been at a school for at least three days.

Swept up in the spectacle of our first flag-raising assembly on the Pathum Thani Prep playground, I thought, "I can do this." Each subsequent morning, assembly grows more familiar and the songs and dances get easier. I'm learning from the teachers and from the children. Next week, when Steve and I are supposed to lead the assembly, I'll be doing the Pinocchio with the best of them. Singing and dancing are decidedly *not* part of Steve's skill set, but he's making a valiant effort to keep up and keep smiling here in the Land of Smiles.

But when we go inside and the school day begins in earnest, our comfort levels flip-flop. When it comes to teaching lessons, Steve is faring pretty well. He knows a thing or two about classroom management. After all, he has a master's degree in elementary education and taught fifth grade for a few years after leaving government. I'm struggling mightily and am not convinced I can pull this off.

Miranda's weekly schedules for K1 (the two- and

three-year-olds) and K2 (age four) are kaleidoscopic works of art, color-coded for the four Prep teachers (Miranda/green, Candace/orange, Steve/blue, and me/yellow) and three special-subject instructors from the *rong rian*, the main school in the old building across the playground from Prep. Miranda and Candace teach math, geography, gardening, cooking, and art lessons for K1 and K2. Miranda (and only Miranda) runs the daily Montessori hour. Laoshi Ling (red) comes for Chinese on Tuesdays and Fridays, the lovely Khru Nok (purple) gives Thai lessons Mondays and Wednesdays, and swim lessons are Thursday mornings. There is no recess or free time, though the K1 kids get forty minutes to nap after lunch.

What jumps out from the color-coded schedules is that most of Steve's blue blocks are on the K2 page, and most of my yellow blocks are with K1. Does Miranda think I have some magical mothering instincts that will make me a natural with the youngest children? Well, I don't.

On our first day, Miranda asks me to shadow Candace in K1. Candace is a capable, warm-hearted young woman from Cape Town, with generous curves and corkscrew curls. The K1 kids, all three of them, adore her. She's chattier than Miranda and took time to explain how the classroom is organized, personal details about each student, and enough of her own backstory to make me think that she would have fit right in with our 23andWe gang in Chiang Mai. If teaching in Thailand gives that group the poise and self-assurance it has given Candace, they'll have done all right for themselves.

The morning goes quickly with milk time, toilet time, a flashcard lesson on shapes and colors, and Chinese squeezed in before lunch, and I begin to understand how this school, or maybe every kindergarten, operates. It's all about language immersion. Whether the language is English, Chinese, or body language, the children soak it up. It must work, because the K1s respond to Candace like they've heard English their whole lives.

Lunch that first day is steamed rice, scrambled eggs, and pork stir-fry. While the kids wash their dishes, standing on chairs to reach the kitchen sink and splashing water everywhere in true Montessori style, Steve and I compare notes.

Steve reports that K2 has been busy too. Miranda taught geography using a puzzle map of Asia. Half the kids (there are eight—Ivy and seven little boys) could name most of the countries.

"Wow, I couldn't," I say. "Could you?"

"As puzzle pieces, Laos looked a lot like Vietnam," Steve admits. "But one boy, Golf—cute name, huh—he knew them all, and their capital cities. I'd never even heard of the capital of Myanmar. Wasn't it Rangoon?"

"Not Mandalay?" I say. "Is that a real place, or did Kipling make it up?" Argh! At least my K1s won't be so academically challenging. I hope.

After lunch, everyone crowds into the bathroom, an open-plan arrangement of six knee-high toilets and two trough sinks, located between the two classrooms. Miranda soon herds the K2s off for math, and Candace is keen to show me the naptime routine.

"They brush their teeth, then I get them changed," she explains as she unrolls a sleep set—miniature quilt with matching pillow attached—for each K1 student.

Chompoo is first out of the bathroom and into the storage area that doubles as a changing room. Candace gets Chompoo's pink pajamas from her pink rolling backpack, unbuttons the two-year-old's shirt, helps her out of her school uniform, buttons up her pajamas, and announces, "Naptime, time to sleep," sending Chompoo to her quilt.

Next comes Panit, happy to let his teacher unbutton and remove his shirt, soaking wet from his enthusiastic toothbrushing. "Naptime, time to sleep," Candace tells him, and Panit runs to his quilt. Sai is last, and I watch in admiration as Candace efficiently dispatches her to nap. But by the time Sai's head hits her pillow there's a glitch—Chompoo has joined Panit on his quilt and the two are giggling over some shared secret. Forty minutes later only Sai has slept, but now the whole procedure has to be repeated in reverse. Pajamas come off, uniforms go on, and beds are rerolled and stowed for tomorrow. The afternoon is another blur of activities—lessons, story time, circle time, dismissal, and, until the kids' rides arrive, playground time.

The next day, Miranda asks me to read for K1's story time, my first time leading a class. Surprisingly, it's slim pickin's on the bookshelves in this otherwise well-equipped school, but there's a large-format picture book featuring a big yellow dog. It's not Kipper or Clifford or Biscuit, and there are no words, but I can spin a tale for Sai, Panit, and Chompoo, can't I?

I sit with the kids on the tiled floor and, starting with the cover illustration, ask them what they see. No response.

"Is this a dog?" I say. No answer.

"Arf, arf?" Still nothing.

"Bau, bau?" I try, resorting to Italian. What do Thai dogs say, anyway?

The children apparently don't know, either. Or maybe my American English is too unfamiliar. Panit stands up and goes to the stack of wooden cubes, part of the untouchable (except under Miranda's supervision) Montessori materials. While I try to steer Panit back to the group, Sai declares, "I need to use the toilet." It takes Miranda's intervention to pull Panit away from the blocks and to get Chompoo away from the abacus, another off-limits item. Who can blame them, though? Wouldn't anyone rather play with nicely crafted, stimulating toys than listen to a strange lady make up a story about a rather dull dog?

After lunch—steamed rice, scrambled eggs, and chicken stir-fry—Chompoo once again is the first to emerge from tooth-brushing, and Candace asks me to change her clothes.

"Chompoo," I ask the girl, so tiny her whole body could eas-ily fit inside her backpack, "can you unbutton your shirt?" She tilts her head as if unsure how to answer, and I can't tell whether it's my English or the notion of undressing independently that puzzles her. "Would you like to try?" She tilts to the other side, her dark eyes looking straight into mine, which I decide to inter-pret as a yes. "Look, it's easy. Just push the button through the hole."

With my fingers guiding hers, Chompoo manages one but-ton then another. The last is at her collar, too hard to see. "Good job, Chompoo," I tell her, as together we get her pajamas on. "Now naptime, time to sleep."

On her quilt, Chompoo fiddles with her pajama buttons. On his quilt, Panit observes her intently. By the end of naptime, Chompoo has all but the topmost button of her pajamas open.

Miranda doesn't ask me to teach any classes in the afternoon. I watch her teach the K2s how to position mung beans on damp cotton balls in a jar and explain how we'll observe them as they germinate in the coming days. She has eight children in her thrall. I watch Steve review the map of Asia. The kids seem even more fascinated with him than with the mung beans. He even manages to keep Golf from shouting out the country names, at least some of the time. And I watch Candace with her color and shape flashcards, handing each card over to the child who gets the right answer, then collecting them and starting all over again till everyone knows everything. Can I imagine myself doing any of this? Not for a second.

On the magic Day Three, Steve and I arrive at school just as Chompoo's grandparents, about our age, are walking her to the gate. All the adults *wai*, then Chompoo's grandmother presses Chompoo's hands together to make the greeting.

"You are Teacher Dian?" The grandmother's face lights up as her husband translates my much-too-lengthy reply about how happy we are to be here and what a bright child Chompoo is. Then she kneels down and says something in Thai to Chompoo.

Chompoo tilts her head, answers with a laugh, and proceeds to unbutton her shirt. Then, with her grandmother's hands guiding Chompoo's, they button the five little buttons from the waistband up to the collar.

"*Khop khun kha*, Teacher Dian," says the grandmother. Before her husband has a chance to translate, I reply, "*Mai pen rai*—It's nothing."

"Score one for Teacher Dian!" Steve says, as we walk with Chompoo down the alphabet path to the classroom—*A a ant, B b bee, C c cat,* all the way to *Z z zebra*—taking care not to step on any animals.

We'll see what else Day Three brings, but as of this morning, with Chompoo's clever little hand in mine, I'm still willing to give Prep a chance.

Pathum Thani Morning Glory

We survived our first three days. Though we had envisioned a very different experience teaching in Thailand, we kept our position at Pathum Thani Prep because the school director, Dr. Pat, offered three attractive perks: a job-sharing arrangement, a convenient and practically rent-free apartment, and use of the swimming pool at the *rong rian*.

To us, job-sharing meant each of us would split our days, half in the classroom and half reading and drinking sweet, strong Thai iced coffee in the nearby café. One morning early in our tenure at Prep we took our first, and last, coffee break. During Laoshi Ling's Chinese lesson, we walked down the alphabet path, continued along the *soi* that runs between the *rong rian* and our apartment building, and gazed across the highway to Café Noah.

We don't know the name of the highway or if it even has a name. All we know is that its eight lanes carry a constant stream of traffic; we hear it in the classroom during school hours and in our bedroom all night long. With no traffic signals anywhere nearby, crossing involves waiting for an opening, an all-out sprint to the overgrown median, and a second dash to relative safety on the other side.

The two young baristas were delighted to have customers— the empty café is the only business on this stretch of highway that opens before evening, when the street food vendors set up shop—and to learn our story. We were happy to tell them, because the coffee was excellent and we had every intention of becoming regulars. Café Noah would be the place where everyone knew our names. And our iced coffee orders.

That afternoon, we learned that Dr. Pat had a different concept of job-sharing. She was out of town, but word of our adventure reached her, the way word of all our adventures would become common knowledge in the months ahead.

"The *rong rian* teachers don't know about your job-share arrangement," Dr. Pat's deputy, the intimidating principal of the *rong rian*, explained to Miranda, who in turn had to explain to us. "They won't understand if they see you leave Prep during the school day. Better if you stay and help around school when you aren't teaching lessons," she said.

I'm learning that messages that might cause even the slightest bit of discomfort are generally communicated via a game of telephone. We've just gone from job-sharing to full-time teachers with no coffee breaks and, unless we want to play telephone in reverse, no avenue for appeal.

Our day starts at 7:30 with gate duty: greeting each kindergartner, taking their temperature (though no one has been sick), and skipping them down the alphabet path to the classroom. From 8 a.m. until 3 p.m. we are in full kindergarten immersion, teaching or assisting the other teachers with everything from lessons to lunch to naptime. After school we have playground duty.

Possibly, we've been assigned gate and playground duties out of kindness: they are easier than overseeing the early arrivals eating breakfast and teaching the after-school enrichment sessions. But outdoors in the heat, even early in the morning, and even in the shade, I wilt. So I see the swimming pool at the *rong rian*, across the *soi* from our apartment, as our deliverance. But will that also prove illusory?

On Friday afternoon, after our first week teaching, we change and head straight to the pool. Yesterday Steve was in the water with the children during their swim lesson, but this is my first look. The pool is stunning—five blue-tiled, twenty-five-meter lanes under a sun canopy, frangipani trees bordering the deck. And filled with children, a half dozen per lane, rhythmically kick-kick-kick-boarding to a coach's encouraging commands.

Seeing our swimsuits and towels, the coach explains, mostly through body language, that Swim Academy meets every day after school, and he needs all the lanes. Workouts end at 7:00 p.m., right around dusk. When the last swimmer departs, he locks the gate.

Unwilling to ask the mysterious telephone network for clarification of the pool policy, we inquire with our neighbors in the apartment building. None of the teachers from Thailand has ever dipped her toes in the water. Maybe they know enough about what little children do in the pool, or how it is maintained, to keep their distance, but they don't share any of that with us, and we don't ask. What we don't know can't hurt us, if we ever do manage to get in the water.

Two of the more intrepid Filipina teachers used the pool once, but that was during a school break, when the students were gone. From their giggles, we get the impression that their dip was a one-time escapade, done on a dare.

The Chinese teachers have yet to use the pool. Both would like to join the children's Swim Academy, but they can't because they have afternoon school bus duty.

"Don't you have bus duty?" Laoshi Ling asks. "I thought all the teachers had bus duty a few days a week." A good question, one that hadn't crossed our minds until now. We file this information under "special treatment." Like our gate and playground assignments, it makes us suspect that, in some ways, life is easier for us than for the other teachers.

Our apartment is another item in the file. It's far from luxurious by American standards. The building's utilitarian design and simple decor, not to mention the youth of most of the residents, remind us of student housing, and Steve has taken to calling our building "the dorm." But did all the teachers get new furniture and flooring when they moved in? This week, a washing machine was installed on the ground floor for all to use. Where did the others do their laundry before our arrival? In their kitchen sinks, we presume, because even Pee Wee, the building caretaker, needed my help to operate the machine.

I was glad for the chance to help Pee Wee, who didn't know quite what to make of an American couple in their sixties moving into her building. Until our arrival, all the other tenants were single, female teachers under thirty. We, in turn, don't know if we should follow our young neighbors' example and address her as *pee*, the honorific for an older person, or if she should accord us that title. We can't ask her directly—our limited Thai is not up to such a delicate question. We deem it safest to render her full respect, in case our toilet ever clogs or, worse yet, our bedroom air-conditioning unit conks out.

On Saturday morning before daybreak, the campus is empty. Maybe the pool is empty, too? The only sound we hear above the relentless highway traffic is the rhythmic swish-scritch, swish-scritch, swish-scritch of Pee Wee's straw broom sweeping the alley of the night's leaf fall.

We don our swimsuits, walk outside, and wave and *wai* to Pee Wee at the other end of the *soi*. Hopefully, we approach the pool gate and Steve pulls the padlock.

"Locked," he sighs. But I'm not ready to give up and, after rattling the padlock myself, suggest we check for another entrance. The main gate to the *rong rian* is the only other possibility, and it too is locked. Disappointed, we turn to cross the *soi* to the dorm.

And there she is, ready to make good on Dr. Pat's promise. Pee Wee approaches, key in hand, to open the pool gate and admit us to what, this morning, will pass for paradise in Pathum Thani.

As the days pass, we realize that Pee Wee sweeps the *soi* before sunrise seven days a week. Most mornings, we set our alarm for 5:15. And most mornings we find the padlock on the gate carefully positioned to look locked. But it isn't. We swim and add the soft slap of our freestyle to the rhythm of Pee Wee's broom on the *soi*. I like to think that she shares our sense of contentment as we greet the glory of the sunrise together.

To Market, To Market

Today we venture forth! The groceries the General bought us on our first day in Pathum Thani are long gone. So are those we got when Candace introduced us to what will surely become a regular destination—a shopping mall (known here as a "lifestyle center") called Robinson. Shopping bags in hand, we stand on the gravelly shoulder of the highway to flag a taxi for our first unassisted ride in Pathum Thani. We have a cheat sheet with helpful hints from Candace on what to tell the driver, how much to pay (sixty-five baht, tops), and landmarks along the route, the main one being the bridge across Thailand's principal artery, the Chao Phraya River, into neighboring Nonthaburi province.

Within seconds, a Toyota taxi—canary yellow on top, parrot green on the bottom—pulls over. The driver opens the window, and Steve greets him with the standard, "*Sawaddee khrap,*" and gives our destination, "Robinson *khrap.*" The driver is puzzled. Steve repeats, "Robinson *khrap.*" The driver remains mystified.

I give it a go. "RobinSOHN *kha.*" A look of understanding, then a smile, cross his face and he repeats, "RobinSOHN *khrap,*" changing the feminine polite particle to the masculine and, more importantly, stressing the final syllable, as Thai people usually do when pronouncing English words and names. We're on the road.

"You teacher?" (pronounced tea-CHER), asks the driver.

"Yes, we're English teachers, from America," Steve answers.

"Teacher! Very good!" Our driver seems genuinely pleased to have us in his cab.

Steve keeps an eye on the meter to ensure we don't pass our destination, five kilometers from home, while I attempt small talk. The roadside scenery, open-air businesses and street food vendors, is neither memorable nor lovely, until we reach a truss bridge. The view from the top—a glittering, orange-roofed *wat* on the curvaceous bank of the wide, brown river—reminds us we are in Thailand. A few minutes later we pull up in front of Robinson. We pay with a one-hundred-baht note, though tips aren't expected, in celebration of our maiden voyage.

"Success!" I say with a high five to Steve. "But how did the driver know we were teachers?"

"Well, he did pick us up right in front of school," Steve says. Sometimes I am oblivious to the obvious.

Luckily, we've been dropped off at the entrance to Tops, the mall's colossal grocery store. Grocery shopping has never been my strong suit, and the bigger the store, the more likely I am to emerge with a splitting headache and sans half the items on my list. The technical term for this is "decision fatigue," but in our family it's known as getting stuck in frozen foods, the department most likely to bewilder me with too many tempting choices.

But tonight I have high hopes of success. Our list is short. The freezer section of our fridge is half the size of a shoebox and already encrusted with frost. For better or worse, the frozen food aisle is a no-go zone.

We adopt a divide-and-conquer strategy—Steve will hunt for a broom and cleaning supplies, while I gather the true necessities, food and water. I'm quickly overwhelmed by the selection of bottled water—not a luxury item in Thailand, where tap water is not safe to drink—and I'm still comparing prices and brands when Steve arrives, his mission accomplished. He looks at my empty shopping cart, rolls his eyes, grabs two eight-bottle packages, and dumps them into our cart.

"Come. Let's find the sa-nacks," Steve says, imitating the two-syllable way our students say the word. We find this bit of Thinglish unobjectionable, in fact kind of cute, just as we accept the kids' pronunciation of Teacher Sa-teve.

The sa-nack selection is almost as daunting as the water choices, with offerings from all over Asia. Steve, a junk food connoisseur, wants to try Thai treats. He picks pretzel sticks with spicy *tom yum* flavoring, peanuts produced in Pathum Thani, and a bag of fried crickets. Just in case, I toss in a half dozen each of Snickers and granola bars.

I thrill to find Illy brand espresso, imported from Italy, until Steve reminds me that we have no way to brew it. We've committed to make do with the appliances in the apartment—mini-refrigerator, toaster, and electric kettle—so we reluctantly take a jar of instant Red Cup. With bread for toast, jam, cheese, and several fresh mangoes, we have breakfast in hand.

At checkout, the cashier smiles and says something in Thai that sounds like *bawongawon*, gesturing with one hand then the other and repeating the word. We put on our friendly-help-less-puppy faces, and I manage to say, "*Mai khao jai kha.*" The most widely applicable of my memorized Thai phrases, it means, "I don't understand." The cashier holds up a finger and leaves with the mangoes. Just like at Lotus, our mangoes have been confiscated.

"*Mai khao jai kha,*" I repeat to no one in particular.

A minute later, she returns with another shopping cart containing sixteen more bottles of water, another package of Pathum Thani peanuts, and the mangoes, now in a plastic bag with a sticker showing their weight and price.

"Too much!" I say, but Steve gets the picture. This supermarket uses "buy one get one free" marketing, and I apparently missed the signs.

Dinnertime! Up to now, our street food meals have been hit-or-miss. Without the benefit of printed menus, ordering is largely a matter of pointing at raw ingredients and waiting to see and taste whatever the chef makes. We've had some delicious meals and some disastrous ones, the latter mostly attributable to overly enthusiastic use of chili peppers. Most evenings, we are the only people on the plastic stools beside the outdoor kitchens across the highway from the dorm. We watch other customers arrive on scooters and motorcycles, place orders, pay, and leave with their dinners without ever dismounting, so we never get a glimpse of what they order or what options might be available.

But here in air-conditioned comfort, Tops offers a *farang*-friendly food court version of street food. A dozen vendors serve up Thai specialties, with photos and descriptions in Thai, and sometimes English, taped to the glass separating the chefs from the customers. Steve goes for a roast pork dish and I try a vegetable broth with noodles. We both specify *mai ped*, not spicy, and are delighted to find that these cooks take us seriously.

As we finish the last spoonfuls of our dinners, Steve says, "Do you realize we are the only *farangs* here?" We've not seen another Westerner since we arrived in Pathum Thani, but we had thought this shopping center in the exurbs of Bangkok, with its Starbucks, McDonald's, and Pizza Company, might attract some. We are obviously outsiders here, and yet we've experienced no overt discrimination. So far, being the only *farangs* in Pathum Thani hasn't been a problem; in fact, it's been rather pleasant.

"Yes," I say, "but with a little help from the locals, we're doing fine. We should celebrate our success."

"My sentiments exactly, and I see just the spot." Steve points to a red sign just outside the Tops, and my jaw drops. I'm not homesick for conversation with my countrymen, but here's a bit of America that I can't resist. DQ!

I order two ten-baht cones and could practically kiss the cheerful, uniformed teenager who understands me perfectly. The vanilla custard tastes exactly like it does at home and like it has since we were children. Ahh, frozen foods. The perfect ending to an evening out in Thailand.

Housewarming

"Please come Tuesday evening at 7:00 for drinks and dessert," reads the invitation I tape to each apartment door. Most of the teachers we work with at Prep commute to school, but some of the teachers at the adjacent *rong rian* live with us on campus. It's time we got to know our dorm mates.

Over the past two weeks some have said hello and introduced themselves, and I've had a few brief conversations. But I haven't exchanged much more than a *wai* with most of them, and remembering their names has been a challenge. All are Asian women, all have long black hair, and all wear the teacher uniform—black skirt or slacks and a polo shirt with the *rong rian's* insignia on the left breast. I'm mildly jealous of their shirts, and not just because they fit and flatter the teachers' youthful figures so nicely. Unlike Prep's acrid orange, the *rong rian's* uniforms are a pretty shade of lavender I'd be happy to put on each morning.

The party is as good an excuse as we'll get for gussying up our apartment, so I tape a map of Thailand to our whitewashed walls and, inspired by kindergarten, make construction-paper chains as swag window treatments. The menu requires some thought, as party menus always do.

Every autumn for the past twenty years or so, Steve and I have hosted an open house for our neighbors, and I'm a little sad to miss 2019. At home, I begin mulling over the menu months in advance. Nothing too fancy, just something special because it's homemade. We've had brunches with waffles, muffins, or bagels; pudding parties and pie parties; pretzel and beer fests; and the ever-popular cookies and cocoa. We always have a cauldron of spiced apple cider on the stove, which fills the house with the cinnamon scent of autumn and puts everyone in a Thanksgiving mood.

Even if we had a stove, serving hot cider in Pathum Thani would be like serving slushies in Siberia. Without an oven we can't bake, either. Somehow the dorm girls don't strike me as a wine and cheese crowd. This is a good call. I'll later read in a memoir by Senator Tammy Duckworth, whose mother is Thai, that cheese triggers the gag reflex in many Thai people. So though it's practically against my religion to do so, we'll serve American-style refreshments straight from the supermarket— Oreos, Pepperidge Farm cookies, fruit, and punch.

Promptly at seven o'clock, our guests arrive en masse, as if someone has coordinated all the residents. Several bring chairs, correctly assuming we don't have seating for everyone, and two dozen bodies squeeze into our living room. "Oooh, what beautiful furniture," says one young woman, admiring our eye-popping, candy-apple red vinyl love seats.

"Thanks so much for coming," I say once everyone gets settled. "I'm Dian, and this is Steve, and we're the new kindergarten teachers at Prep. How about you?" Around the room, each teacher says her name and what grade she teaches at the *rong rian*.

It soon becomes clear from their accents that they have arranged themselves like delegations to an international conference. Ling, whom we already know as the Chinese teacher at Prep, sits beside her roommate Ting. A group of teachers from

Thailand cluster on and around one loveseat, a larger group from the Philippines around the other. It's now confirmed that we are the only Westerners, and the only old folks (apart from Pee Wee, who hasn't joined us), and Steve is the only male, in the building.

Teacher Reyna, fluent in English, assumes the role of spokeswoman, and I guess that she coordinated the punctual entrance. She explains that most of the teachers hail from the same small city in the Philippines.

"We all went to the local teacher's college, and one by one, by word of mouth, came to Pathum Thani." When asked why, she explains, "It's hard to find jobs back home. Here the pay is better, and we can send money to our families."

"Do you like living in Thailand?" Steve asks.

"It's good. People in Pathum Thani are friendly, and the children are sooooo sweet," Reyna says. Steve's eyebrows and my own rise in synchrony. "But it's hard to be so far from home. I haven't seen my parents and brothers in three years." Steve and I both nod sympathetically. We won't be separated from our own family more than six months.

Perhaps shyness or perhaps their English makes the Thai teachers quieter than the Filipinas. I ask them to show us their hometowns on the map. The borders of Thailand look like an elephant's head and trunk, and most of the teachers point to one of the ears, either northern Thailand or Isaan in the northeast. A few can find their hometowns, but most describe their villages relative to features significant enough to appear on the map. I suppose the Thai teachers, like our Filipina colleagues, live in the dorms to economize and help their families far from the capital.

We've now met all the neighbors except one—the mangy-looking dog that is a near-constant presence in the *soi* and that I assiduously avoid.

"Does anyone feed him?" Steve asks.

"Is he tame?" I ask.

"That's my buddy Jake," Reyna says cheerfully. "He's a stray, but he hangs out here. He's perfectly safe. And he loves my chicken adobo."

"We call him Tarlo," say several Thai teachers, nearly in unison. Both the Thai and Filipina teachers have adopted the mutt, and I'm happy to hear he is well cared for. I'm even happier to know he doesn't bite, though I wonder about the availability of rabies vaccines in Pathum Thani, both for him and for us.

Our fruit punch is a huge hit. "How did you make it?" asks Ling. She giggles upon hearing we added sparkling wine, and I take her and a few others to refill the pitcher. They marvel at the size of our table-space kitchen.

"Aren't all the apartments the same?" I ask. I've wondered about this. Our three-room flat—living room, bedroom, and kitchen, with the outdoor bathroom on the balcony—makes sense for a couple. But these are all single women. Do roommates share a bedroom?

"Oh, no," says Teacher Reyna. "Our units are divided into three bedrooms, with a teeny tiny space for cooking. This place was fixed up just for you."

"We have to eat standing up, with our bowls on top of the refrigerator," Ting says. "And look at your floor. So beautiful!"

Our floor is concrete covered with thin plastic sheeting. Since we arrived, some of the tape holding the sheeting together has already worn away, and a layer of dirt and (mostly) dead insects has accumulated underneath. Ting opens the chest-high fridge and marvels at the ice in the miniature tray. Her smaller, older refrigerator barely keeps food cool, even in the freezer section.

If our apartment is a sign of preferential treatment, we've

done nothing to deserve it, and it makes us a bit uncomfortable. We wonder if it's a privilege of age or of being American. Fortunately, no one seems to resent our good luck, or they are too polite to show it.

At nine o'clock on the dot, taking their cue from Reyna, everyone readies to leave. At the door, the Thais smile and *wai*, and the Filipinas give us hugs.

I sweep up cookie crumbs as a precaution against the nightly ant invasion, Steve gathers up paper cups, and we both try to match names with faces and stories. We will be lucky to get half of them right.

"But who could forget Ting 'n Ling?" Steve says. These two have captured my imagination, too. Over the coming months, we'll get to know them better. In some ways, Ting and Ling share a lot in common with Steve and me. They are the only teachers from China, and we are the only Americans. Like us, they share an apartment and spend most of their free time with each other. But they work much harder. While we have eleven students at Prep, they are responsible for several hundred kids at the *rong rian*, which includes K1, K2, K3, and six elementary grades. A few times each week, they have to wake up before dawn to ride the morning school bus and stay late for the afternoon ride home. In Pathum Thani traffic, Ling says, the rides are often more than an hour.

They are recent college graduates, part of a small army of volunteer Chinese-language teachers in Thailand sponsored by the Chinese government. Their monthly stipend is less than our weekly pay, which just about covers the basic necessities of life in Pathum Thani, so both Ling and Ting earn spending money by tutoring. I'm guessing many of the other teachers also have tutoring gigs so they can send more generous remittances home.

The warmth of the Chinese teachers' friendship impresses me, as does the jolly camaraderie of the Filipinas and the quieter closeness of the Thai teachers. But I'm a little saddened by the tribalism that the dorm assignments—in every apartment, all the roommates come from the same country—seem to foster. I worry that this is our fate, too.

In the months ahead, my worry will prove well founded. Along with the special treatment we seem to be accorded, being here as a married couple, a much older married couple, will set us apart from our neighbors. So will my lower tolerance for the heat, bugs, and other physical discomforts of Pathum Thani and our resulting weekend escapes to Bangkok.

On my way to the dorms' oil-drum trash cans, I encounter Tarlo/Jake sprawled on the pavement in his usual spot. "The girls take good care of you, don't they?" I ask softly, heeding the ever-sound advice about sleeping dogs. It must be easy to make friends when you're traveling solo.

What's on the Agenda?

Children are scattered on the playground when Steve and I call out, "Time to go home." Some are on the jungle gym, some are pushing toy wheelbarrows around the running track, and some are creating a dinosaur hatchery under the frangipani tree, nestling egg-shaped rocks into a mound of petals. I don't like rushing the kids. This half hour after dismissal is the only unstructured part of their day. But today they need to go home on time. Today we have a staff meeting.

Usually, we can round everyone up with ease, except Panit. Panit is fast—his little legs are all muscle. Though drenched in sweat after several dozen laps with the wheelbarrow, he has no intention of stopping. Most days we lure Panit off the track with a game of hide-and-seek. But today Steve scoops up the hot, damp boy to deliver him bodily to his grandma.

During the school day, Panit is the bane of my K1 existence. If I ask the class to sit, Panit runs off. Once Panit runs off, the two girls, Chompoo and Sai, are sure to follow. Actually, they don't follow, they run in different directions. Corralling them is hopeless, and my lesson plans are pointless.

The situation is embarrassing and demoralizing. The class is tiny, in terms of both body count and body mass. I weigh more than my three elfin charges combined. Why can't I keep them in their seats for a forty-minute lesson?

Sometimes when Panit runs off, it's to the toilet, and I surely won't deny him that. But he still wears pull-up Pampers and, I'm told, requires supervision in the bathroom. Until now, Miranda or Candace has been around to help, leaving me blissfully alone with the girls. Today, they weren't, and I decided to let Panit poop solo.

When Panit announced, "Finished now," I went to the bathroom, congratulated him, and told him to put his Pampers and shorts back on and return to the classroom. He didn't. He kept sitting on the pot and announcing, "Finished now," until his pride turned to frustration, then to fear. I had no idea what to do, until Sai came to my rescue.

"Time to wash," she said, handing me the closest bum gun.

I passed the spray handle to Panit and watched to see how he'd manage. Not well. The result was water everywhere, wet shorts, tears streaming down Panit's face, and the girls left to their own devices in the classroom while I mopped up.

Miranda and Candace are masters of classroom management. They've seen the chaos in my classes and a few times have intervened to help. But we've yet to have an in-depth conversation about the children, the curriculum, and my growing frustration at my inability to maintain control.

Instead, Steve and I conduct our own nightly therapy sessions. Our conversations mostly focus on K1 and mostly involve Steve trying to pep me up. Our only reference point is our daughter's experience more than twenty years ago. This preschool—because K1 really is more of a preschool than a kindergarten—is nothing like what we remember. Rose had to be toilet trained before we could enroll her. Her "classes" consisted mostly of playtime, with a little singing, story time, and art sprinkled in. Any exposure she got to glitter happened at preschool. Any exposure she got to the three Rs happened at home. Here our young charges have a string of academic lessons every day, each with its associated workbook.

Having handed the children to their families, Steve and I go inside and join our colleagues around the kid-sized purple table.

Candace begins by saying, "Dian, you seem to be frustrated. What can we do to help?" Miranda is looking in any direction but mine. She may be the head teacher, but she's quite content to let Candace take the lead here.

I take a deep breath. I'm itching to itemize my ideas for making my life, and the children's lives, happier at Prep. Cut back on the formal lessons. Let the kids play more. Let them explore the Montessori materials more, rather than treating them like display objects. Ditto books. Read the kids more stories. Oh, and insist students be out of diapers before admitting them to school.

But I know these are all culturally insensitive nonstarters. At our orientation in Chiang Mai, Mark repeatedly told us to experience the Thai educational system, not try to change it. Keep cool and smile.

Swallowing hard, I ask, "How do you keep the kids' attention?"

"Oh, they're just testing their limits with you. Give it time," Candace says.

"How long did it take you to gain their respect?" I ask.

That's when we learn that both Miranda and Candace have been at Prep since it opened two years ago as a school within a school. They've forged a partnership and a friendship. And they've developed relationships with the students and their parents that are stronger than any Steve or I will ever achieve. Candace was new to teaching, but Miranda, an experienced teacher at the *rong rian* next door, was recently trained in Montessori teaching methods.

"I joined Prep to put the Montessori philosophy into practice," Miranda says, "not to be the head teacher. But that's what Dr. Pat needed, so here I am."

This isn't a good omen. Sometimes, it's a gift to have a manager who isn't into management. For most of my career in science, my bosses were more interested in doing their own research than managing their employees. The freedom they gave me led to fruitful research, thanks to nearly a decade of graduate school training and mentors to guide me in my early years. That model isn't going to work here.

"Don't worry," says Miranda. "Just show them you love them."

In the evening, I don't know whether to laugh or fume at the uselessness of our afternoon session.

"Cut them some slack," Steve says. "Neither of them has much trouble with classroom management. Maybe you can learn a thing or two from them. As for supervising, Miranda is doing the best she knows how"

"So am I," I wail. "Unfortunately, the best I know how isn't near good enough. I could do better if..." and I tick off all the items I didn't tick off during our meeting.

"None of those are things you control. They're all way above your pay grade."

Above my pay grade. Do people use that term outside government? At my federal job, I hated the phrase, a stock response from bureaucrats, budgeteers, and even top banana executives to any problem they couldn't or wouldn't solve. There were other things I didn't like about government service, but one thing I *did* like was staff meetings.

Most everyone in our lab was an introverted scientist. We

could stay happily occupied all day with the minimum of human interaction. Without our monthly staff meetings, communication with our colleagues might not amount to much more than a polite greeting in the morning and, possibly, a wave goodbye at the end of the day.

I brought my respect for workplace meetings into our home. When Rose was about ten and her after-school activities started interfering with family dinners, we designated Friday evenings as family meeting nights, not to be missed on any account. We had an agenda, and all three of us were required to speak to each agenda item.

Item I – How was your week?

Item II – What's coming up in the week ahead?

Item III – What's on your mind?

The true value of this routine became apparent when Rose reached her teens. Friday dinners became the only time in the week when our conversations went beyond the purely practical.

I'd happily delay the start of our weekend to have a regular Friday afternoon confab with Miranda and Candace, our Prep family. We could even use the same agenda that worked for the Seidel family. But I'm not going to suggest it. That's way above my pay grade.

I'll just have to continue watching Miranda and Candace and hope some of their competence rubs off on me. But at least I can share my many problems and rare successes with Steve during our daily decompression sessions over dinner. Our agenda is simple—good old Item III—What's on your mind?

I Love You, Teacher Steve

"What are you teaching the big kids today?" I ask Steve as I spread mango jam on toast. "No, wait, let me guess. Past simple and past continuous tenses?"

"Big kids? Very funny," he replies, slicing a finger-length, supersweet banana on his granola. "Try baby animals and their homes. We'll play a matching game with picture cards. Then they'll make baby birds and nests out of clay."

"Well, that sounds kind of fun." I'm actually a little jealous of Steve's schedule. The K2s don't need assistance at the toilet, though how Steve manages eight kids is beyond me.

"Everything *sounds* fun," he says. "But if Athit's in class, all bets are off."

"Which one is Athit again?" I ask.

"The tall, gangly boy with the permanent scowl on his face."

It takes me a moment to conjure Athit's image. He's been absent a lot.

"Oh, I know who you mean," I say. "But he seems more sad to me than angry."

"You haven't had him in class. Come watch. You'll see."

Until now, Steve and I have agreed to be out of the classroom when the other is teaching, partly to spare each other embarrassment but mainly for a break from the kids. But this morning, I join his K2 class. I roll golf-ball-sized portions of yellow and brown clay at our shared teacher desk while Steve and eight children are in miniature purple plastic chairs squeezed around the matching purple table meant for six.

I'm impressed. Most of the kids are working independently or in impromptu teams, engrossed with the picture cards, unbothered by the tight quarters. Baby bears get matched with caves, ants with hills, and puppies with doghouses. This last pairing must surely be by process of elimination—as far as I can tell, the majority of Thai dogs don't have the luxury of roofs over their heads. Sai, whose recent fourth birthday meant a promotion from K1 to K2, is considering whether a bird lives in a nest or a hive. Steve gently moves a picture of a bee toward her, and her face lights up.

"I love you, Teacher Steve," Sai chirps as she makes the correct matches. A sweet sentiment, but Steve knows not to take it to heart. Sai's "I love you" is sometimes an expression of affection, but it can also be a greeting, or a bid for attention, or simply a chance to hear her own voice speaking English. By the end of most days, she has announced her love for all her classmates and teachers.

Then, for no apparent reason, Athit leaves his purple chair and is en route to the bins of blocks in the rear of the room.

"Athit," Steve says, "this isn't playtime. Please stay here with us."

"Athit," Sai calls, looking up from her animals, "come help me. I love you."

Athit heeds neither appeal.

Steve clears his throat and warns in his stern teacher voice, "Athit, you can sit in a purple chair with the class or the yellow one. Your choice."

Athit looks at Steve, then at Sai, then, eyes narrowing, at

the yellow chair in a corner reserved for kids who need time to regroup. Next he walks directly to the yellow chair and sits deliberately down. Now I see the scowl that Steve described this morning, and it's sad to imagine the grooves it's carving into Athit's smooth brow.

Steve goes to the yellow chair, squats, and quietly tells Athit, "You can sit here until you are ready to join your friends at the table."

By way of reply, Athit announces loudly and with conviction, "I *don't* love you, Teacher Steve."

I'm shocked, but Steve simply sighs in frustration and gives me a look that says, "See what I mean?"

Another boy, Chet, has an expression on his face that pains me almost as much as Athit's behavior seems to have pained Chet. Barely above a whisper and addressing no one in particular, he says, "Teacher Steve loves us. We should love him too."

Taking Chet's cue, Sai whispers, "I love you, Teacher Steve." A chorus of voices echoes the sentiment, first softly, then loudly, until finally Steve has to shush them to refocus their attention on the baby animals.

After all the picture cards have been paired and collected, Steve quizzes the children on the new vocabulary, ending with, "Where does the baby bird live?" and everyone (except Athit) shouts, "In a nest!"

"Right you are! So, let's make some birds, and let's make nests for them to live in." Steve turns to Athit and asks, "Are you ready to join us?"

Athit looks vaguely interested but won't dignify the question with an answer.

"Athit, please bring the clay from Teacher Dian to the table," Steve asks calmly. Again, Athit says nothing and holds his ground. It was worth a try, but now Steve asks Sai and Chet to get the clay and lets Athit remain in the yellow chair.

"Ooooh, choc-o-late!" swoons Sai when I hand her the bowl of brown clay spheres. "I love you, choc-o-late!"

Before she can pop one in her month, Steve shouts, "No, not chocolate. It's clay. You can't eat it."

"Ca-lay," repeats Sai, a bit mournfully.

A teachable moment if I ever saw one. But does Steve see it? We've learned that the last syllable in many Thai words is stressed, which is relatively rare in English. Stressing the first syllable of *chocolate* is hard for Thai people, who often compromise and give all three syllables equal stress.

Then there's clay, with its initial double consonant blend, another problem for Thai speakers, who usually put a vowel sound between the C and L sounds. So much to work with!

But the choc-o-late ca-lay challenge doesn't inspire Teacher Steve. He's just happy the kids aren't eating the art supplies. Twenty minutes later, seven yellow vaguely avian shapes nestle cozily in seven brown cup-shaped nests on the windowsill.

"Congratulations!" I tell Steve. "That was a grand success." I bite my tongue about the missed opportunity for a pronunciation lesson.

"Success? With Athit in the doghouse the whole time?"

"Forget about Athit. Seven out of eight kids did great. Look at these cute little birdies."

"Adorable. But we didn't get ESOL certificates to teach arts and crafts." This kid has rattled Steve, and now it's my turn to do the pepping up.

"Well then, just consider this as grandpa training," I say. "You know what they say about the best part of being a grandparent, right?"

"At the end of the day, you get to send the kids home?"

"Well, okay. And if we ever have a grandson like Athit, we can send him home at lunchtime. But that's not the best part."

"I give up. What?"

"No, don't give up," I say. "Listen to the kids."

Steve shakes his head.

"Then listen to me. I love you, Teacher Steve."

F Is for Frangipani

"Tea-CHER, Pep-PER!" whines Nin. His Thai way of elongating the "-er" parts of both my title and his kindergarten classmate's nickname make Nin sound righteously aggrieved. "Pepper hurt me!"

Nin isn't crying, bleeding, or showing any obvious signs of injury. His is a wail of frustration and exhaustion. I'd wail in frustration and exhaustion, too, if anyone could hear me, but I'm on my own with K2 this morning. Even with a smaller class than usual—Candace has taken Ivy, Golf, and (bless you, Candace) Athit as lunch helpers—things are not going well. Nin's is the third report of Pepper's unsociable behavior this morning.

Sighing, I ask Nin, then Pepper, "What happened?" To color a flower, Pepper needed a purple crayon, the very one Nin was using to color a fish. "Teacher, Pepper just took it. He didn't say, 'May I please'!"

Now I too am aggrieved. Righteously aggrieved. Teaching the kids to ask for things politely in English, instead of saying "I want" (which would be perfectly courteous in Thai), is my biggest classroom achievement to date.

"Pepper," I say, looking straight into his eyes, my hands firm on his shoulders. "What do you think you should do?"

Pepper breaks eye contact, whispers, "Sorry, Nin," and runs to the yellow chair designated for misbehaved students. The rest of the class returns to their purple chairs to complete their letter F coloring pages.

The yellow chair is as familiar territory for Pepper as it is for Athit. But while Athit's misbehavior seems rooted in a dark anger, the source of which I haven't fathomed, Pepper is a sweet, spontaneous child. He is the first to offer a hug to a sad classmate or take a younger student by the hand to cross the playground. But Pepper's loving impulses are bundled with more careless ones that too often leave a classmate in tears.

One morning he arrived at school with a sack of marshmallows to share. At snack time, thrilled to see his friends' eager faces, Pepper handed one to each child, then gobbled his own. A moment later, apparently still hungry, Pepper snatched back a classmate's marshmallow and popped it in his mouth.

A child grabbing sweets isn't front-page news, but it triggered my recollection, from a long-ago college psychology course, of the Mischel marshmallow test. Pepper was just like the four-year-olds in Mischel's laboratory experiment who, when given the choice, could not wait five minutes before eating a marshmallow in order to get a promised second one. That little insight didn't provide any tips for helping Pepper, but it did help me control my own immediate impulse—to send him to the yellow chair, which remains the whole teaching team's default solution to Pepper's outbursts.

After a few minutes I ask, "Pepper, ready to join us at the table? Can you f-f-finish your purple f-f-flower. Can you color the F and stay inside the lines?" Pepper makes a brief attempt, but I've asked too much. All he can manage is to scribble over a few petals.

With all the worksheets more or less completed and the crayon incident behind us, we're all more than ready for lunch.

Unfortunately, lunch isn't ready for us. Candace phones from the kitchen. One of the lunch helpers unplugged the rice cooker, and because a meal without rice is practically an existential crisis in Thailand, Miranda is going to the *rong rian* to see if the cooks there can spare a pot for us. In the meantime, would Steve and I take the kids outside for a while?

Outside? Sure! In the short time we've been here, Steve and I have come to feel that the kids' school day is too long on lessons and too short on free play. The kids, thrilled with the unexpected break from their workbooks and our classroom routine, are running, climbing, and playing hide-and-seek on the playground. Now Pepper is in his element with only a few rules to follow and lines to stay within.

It's only five minutes before I understand why we usually stay indoors. With the sun directly overhead, I'm drenched in sweat and feeling lightheaded. Managing better, Steve offers to watch the kids, who are somehow unbothered by the swelter, while I recover under the shade of a frangipani.

With long, slow breaths, I inhale the softly intoxicating fragrance of the white and yellow flowers—a fruity, spicy blend that, for me, is the defining scent of the tropics.

"Lunchtime!" announce Athit and Ivy, leaning out the kitchen window, and we herd the children onto the alphabet path—*Don't step on Miss Monkey!*—to make our way to the kitchen.

Nin asks, "Where is Pepper?"

My heart starts to race.

The children offer suggestions.

"Look in the bathroom!" says Lek.

"Maybe at the swimming pool," says Sai.

"What if the snake bit him?" Nin seems almost hopeful, but

this isn't the moment for a lesson in compassion and forgiveness. Nor is it time to reckon with our negligence as playground monitors.

All the children's ideas are plausible. Just last week we saw a snake on the playground. Hoping for the most benign location, the bathroom, I shepherd the children back indoors while Steve rushes to hunt the school grounds.

"Don't worry. We'll find Pepper," I say, praying that saying the words aloud will make them true. But he's not in the bathroom, and the yellow chair stands empty in the corner of the classroom.

"Teacher Dian."

I turn and see Pepper at the purple table, a frangipani bloom in his open palm.

"Where did you go?" I cry.

"To find a flower."

"But there are flowers all over the playground! Where did you go?"

"I didn't want a yellow one," he explains. "Here—a purple one—for you."

Was Sai right? Did Pepper cross the *rong rian* campus to the school pool, where purple frangipani trees shade the deck?

After several deep exhales, all I can manage is, "Thank you, Pepper."

"For your ear," he instructs me.

I position the bloom behind my ear and ask, "What do you think you should do now?"

Pepper goes to Nin and arranges a second purple frangipani behind his friend's ear. Then he walks across the classroom and takes his seat in the yellow chair.

Pepper has a lot of work to do on impulse control, and I

suppose my job is to help him. But I'm not a child psychologist, and I have no idea how, or when, to intervene. While often disruptive, his actions are like the fragrance of frangipani—sweet yet complex. But my fundamental responsibility is keeping Pepper and the other kids safe. We both have work to do.

Teacher Training

We'd been at Prep only a few weeks when Miranda informed us of an upcoming school vacation. The calendar showed no national holidays, but we didn't complain about having a week away from the kids to explore Thailand. Dr. Pat clarified the situation.

"We're having teacher training at the *rong rian*," she said. "Please come. Meet the teachers. See how we do things there."

So instead of lounging on a beach or touring the ancient capitals of Siam, we'll finally experience something like a real Thai school. Though all our students are Thai, Pathum Thani Prep uses an "international" curriculum (from Australia, we think), and we teach in English. Like Prep, the *rong rian* on the other side of the playground is a private school, but it follows a Thai curriculum and most classes are in Thai.

And we'll finally see Dr. Pat, who has been away from Pathum Thani most of our brief tenure, in action.

On Monday, we're sitting in a semicircle on a linoleum floor with a score of kindergarten and primary school teachers. Dr. Pat's kickoff lecture, in Thai, is about Italian educator Maria Montessori. I pick up tidbits from the presentation, which features pithy Montessori quotes in English translation. Most of the slides show kids working with what I've learned to call Montessori materials: towers of cubes in a precise progression of sizes; sets of colored beads on linkable wires; panels of fabric with oversized zippers, buttons, laces, and snaps.

We have all this stuff at Prep (although Miranda has been clear that it's only for use during her Montessori lessons), but I don't see any Montessori materials at the *rong rian*. Is Dr. Pat telling us she's introducing Montessori methods here? Or will the *rong rian* teachers bring their classes to Prep this term?

Neither Steve nor I have a clue, and neither of us asks. Above our pay grade.

If we had been placed in a more typical Thai school, would every meeting, training session, and conversation with colleagues be so opaque? Would we, over time and of necessity, learn enough Thai to manage? Or would we be left to our own devices, trusted to teach English but isolated from the rest of the faculty?

I have high hopes of learning something useful in Tuesday morning's session, in English, on lesson planning. In ESOL teacher training in Washington, we learned the basic blueprints of plans for listening, speaking, reading, writing, grammar, and vocabulary lessons. None of that seems relevant to teaching kindergarten, and I'm anxious to know how the pros do their lesson plans.

Our instructor is the school principal, a senior teacher from the Philippines who recruited Miranda and many other teachers from her hometown. For ninety minutes she dictates the elements of a perfect lesson plan: a mandatory font and type size for section headings, a second font for body text, top and side margin measurements, and page number placement. With no further ado or direction, she then informs us that our plans for the remainder of the term are due on Friday.

We are all looking forward to our afternoon with an art teacher from Dr. Pat's school in Bangkok. No one is concerned that she is thirty minutes late—she's an artist, after all. When Dr. Pat learns she's had a minor traffic accident, the art session is canceled.

Steve and I retreat to the Prep classrooms to patch together ten weeks of lessons using workbooks and teaching materials in the classroom and educational websites. Whether I'll be able to teach these lessons in whatever class time is not consumed by chasing children who won't sit still, supervising toileting, and rolling nap quilts remains an open question. But my margins are beyond reproach.

Midmorning Thursday, Dr. Pat appears at Prep.

"Everything okay?" she asks with a disarming smile.

"Would you like to review our plans?" Steve offers.

"No," she laughs, "we just need them for the files, in case the Ministry of Education audits us for accreditation. You can finish them later. Today I'd like you to meet the rest of the faculty."

The second floor of the *rong rian* is a world apart from the kindergarten classrooms below. Student science, art, and geography projects decorate the hallway. Today teachers sit at the neatly arranged desks in a math classroom, but it's easy to imagine well-behaved children calmly completing worksheets and raising their hands to ask permission to use the toilet.

"Please, tell us about yourselves," says Khru Boonmee, the teacher leading the training session for the elementary grade teachers.

"*Sawaddee khrap*," Steve begins. In English, Steve tells the group that we are from America, that we both used to work on environmental issues, and that we'll be teaching at Prep until next March. Several teachers perk up when he mentions his work on the international agreement to protect the ozone layer and as a White House advisor on climate issues.

He fields questions on plastics in the ocean, solar energy, and sea-level rise, tossing the more technical ones my way. At long last, we are in our element, and I'm wondering if Dr. Pat might need a couple of American teachers for English or science classes at the *rong rian*.

"Do you want to introduce yourself?" Khru Boonmee asks me. Of course I do—in Thai. My script comes mainly from our audio course. *My name is Dian. Steve is my husband. We have one daughter. We are from Washington. We are English teachers. Pathum Thani Prep. I am a scientist. I am a yoga teacher. We like Pathum Thani. Thank you.*

Laughter. Applause. The biggest rush I've felt since we arrived in Thailand.

"*Khun poot paasa thai dai dii mak khrap,*" says Khru Boonmee. I'm thrilled both by his overgenerous compliment of my Thai fluency and because I actually understood it.

"*Mai dai kha.*" I hardly need to protest, "I can't." My Thai is toneless and surely painful to the teachers' ears, but Khru Boonmee's words instill hope that someday I might actually deserve them.

"*Dai khrap.* You can," he insists. If I were in fourth grade, I'd want to be in Khru Boonmee's class. In the front row.

"*Nidnoy kha,*" I allow. A little Thai goes a long way. Let's see how far *nidnoy* can get me.

"I know you are all busy teachers," I say, "but if anyone is interested in helping us learn Thai, we'd be happy to help you with English."

Up pops a hand.

"I'd love to!" says a tall slender woman who seems almost as excited by the prospect of a language exchange as I am.

Over the next several months Steve and I will spend our

Thursday evenings with Khru Som. *Som* means "orange." She will teach us other colors and fruits later. We'll finally do what we came here for—teach English. We'll teach her pronunciation, grammar, and vocabulary. We'll practice conversations she might have when she quits working at the *rong rian* and looks for her dream job, teaching *farangs* Thai. Teaching us, she'll have a low-risk chance to give that dream a test ride.

Tonight, I have work to do. I need a lesson plan for our first session with Khru Som. And I'll use whatever margins I damn please.

A Little Thai Lesson

"Ne, neu, no. Nay, ner, noh. Neh, na, naw." In preparation for our second Thai lesson with Khru Som, the science teacher at the *rong rian*, Steve and I recite our homework in unison. I'm not 100 percent sure I'm getting the nine basic vowel sounds right, but I'm 90 percent sure Steve isn't.

"Let's try you repeating after me," I suggest. My lips progress from forced smile to fish face as they emit the first three syllables, "Ne, neu, no."

"No, no, no," Steve articulates, quite clearly. He crosses his forearms, making three big Xs in rhythm with his words.

We both know this bit of Thai body language. In our efforts to communicate with the Pathum Thani locals, we've gotten the message. I order pad thai with shrimp. The street food vendor crosses her arms. *Mai mee*—no shrimp tonight. We tell the taxi driver Bangkok Skytrain. He crosses his index fingers. *Mai dai*—no, I can't go that far.

"It's pointless," Steve complains. "We should be learning practical conversations, not mouthing unpronounceable vowels."

"Khru Som says if we don't learn basic pronunciation, no one will understand a word we say. Please, make a little effort," I plead.

His thumb and forefinger an inch apart, he sighs and says, "A *nidnoy* effort."

"Sawaddee khrap," and *"Sawaddee kha."* Steve and I speak the words to Khru Som, smile, bow our *wai*, and rise in tandem. The *wai* greeting and the smile are the other bits of Thai body language that we know. And love.

Khru Som's first lesson for us was all about the *wai* and the variations required for different social ranks. Our first lesson for her was all about American introductions and handshakes. We didn't know then that by the time we left Thailand Covid-19 would make shaking hands about as acceptable, all around the world, as sneezing in someone's face. From a survival perspective, learning to *wai* might be our most important Thai lesson of all.

Khru Som draws the now-familiar three-by-three grid on the chalkboard, and we spend the next ten minutes reciting the nine vowel sounds in combination with seventeen different consonants. By the time we reach "keh, ka, kaw," Steve's eyes catch mine and dart pointedly to the wall clock and back again.

Torn between my promise not to let our lesson run late and my growing affection for the enthusiastic and intelligent Khru Som, I use a memorized phrase from our audio course to ask her, "Do you want to eat rice?" It takes her a beat or two to decode my dinner invitation, but then her face brightens. "Very good! You speak Thai!"

"Nidnoy," I reply. Sometimes *nidnoy* is enough.

"Too bad Khru Som can't join us," I say as we wait to cross the highway.

"Yes, she could have taught us to order dinner. Now that would be a useful lesson," Steve says, his eyes on the road to avoid my smirk.

Steve and I head to adjacent food stalls for our usual dishes.

"Pad thai goong kha," I say.

The cook nods and repeats, *"Pad thai kha,"* but adds, *"goong mai mee,"* making an X with her forearms. No shrimp tonight.

"Mai pen rai kha," I reply, then translate, "No problem."

In English, she asks, "You like spicy?"

"Nidnoy," I say. I thank her, congratulate myself on another conversational success, and join Steve at a table.

"Go ahead. Enjoy it while it's hot," I say when the *moo ping* chef delivers Steve's skewers of char-grilled pork atop a pile of steaming rice.

My pad thai is a glorious mound of glistening noodles with bean sprouts, peanuts, tamarind sauce, and a wedge of lime. I dig in Thai-style—a fork in my left hand to load the spoon in my right—for a huge bite of a well-earned dinner.

At my gasp, Steve jerks up from his plate. "Drink," he commands, handing me a water bottle.

I push it aside and instead dig an even huger spoonful of his perfectly plain white rice. I swallow, purse my lips, exhale a big breath, and wipe tears from my eyes.

"Did you forget to say not spicy?" he says.

I clear my throat. "Tomorrow we practice *nidnoy.*"

We pack the leftovers—no need to offend the cook—dash back across the highway, and deposit the pad thai in the rusty oil drums that serve as the dorm's trash cans. Upstairs I crank up the AC and sprawl on the bed to monitor the burn moving through my digestive system and reflect on the evening's lessons.

Despite being the only *farangs* at school (and probably the only ones in this corner of Pathum Thani province), we haven't learned much Thai. I enjoy our time with Khru Som, but with her meticulous approach our progress will be painfully slow. I've hardly made a dent in the alphabet, and I still can't distinguish the five basic tones—mid, low, falling, high, and rising—though I know they change word meanings dramatically.

Steve points out that, despite tonight's chili episode, we are managing with *nidnoy* Thai. He is ready to admit defeat. I am not, though I'm losing hope of achieving even an elementary level of proficiency.

Is it time to surrender? No, no, no. Not now, not yet. But a *nidnoy* voice tells me it may be soon.

In Her Shoes

"Come out, come out, wherever you are. Time to go home. It's time to go home." My singsong announcement is for the kindergartners hiding around the playground. I reinforce it by making eye contact with the parents chatting by the school gate, to make it clear that their kids are now their responsibility.

One by one, like fairy elves emerging from their garden hideaways, hidden children reveal themselves, spot their families, and scamper to the gate. Except Sai.

I find the child alone, daydreaming, inside the tube slide. Slowly, reluctantly, she slides down, feet emerging first, shoes on the wrong feet and unfastened.

"Look at your shoes, Sai," I say. "Can you fix them?"

Sai blinks in the sunlight then looks around. Her attention is elsewhere, or nowhere. What is she thinking about?

Mornings I am patient with Sai and give her time to fix her shoes. Her father always drops her off well before the other children arrive, so we have time. Why she can't arrive with her shoes on properly is a mystery I haven't tried to solve.

But this afternoon, it's too hot. I'm too tired. And it is too late, ten minutes past dismissal. This should be my time to breathe, regroup, plan for tomorrow.

"Your shoes, please, Sai. Mommy will be here soon."

"No," she says. Eyebrows raised, I look at her and wait.

"Not Mommy. Papa comes today. To take me to his new house."

I look down at Sai's upturned face. Then I kneel to look her in the eyes. She turns her head to look elsewhere, or nowhere.

I help her switch her shoes and ask, "Does that feel a little better?"

Once more I confront my shortcomings. I don't easily put myself in other people's shoes, especially shoes as small as Sai's. What is my responsibility toward this dreamy, needy child? Is giving her the occasional opportunity to reveal herself enough?

To Bangkok for a Breather

After our first visit to Bangkok twenty-nine years ago, I had no desire to ever return. Though the main tourist sites—the stately Grand Palace, the iconic temples, the bustling marketplaces—were, figuratively speaking, breathtaking, the city air was literally so. On stagnant summer days in Washington we get the occasional "code red" air pollution alert, but only in Bangkok did I understand what L.A. must have been like before the US passed, and enforced, clean air laws.

In 1990, Bangkok's streets were jam-packed with an eye-popping variety of conveyances, each spewing clouds of black exhaust. Tuk-tuks, three-wheeled rickshaws powered by two-stroke engines, filled every road and alley with fumes, smoke, and their puttering "tuk-tuk" percussion. Cars and trucks, lacking the emissions-reducing catalytic converters that have been required in the US since the 1970s, belched filthy clouds of smoke. Smudges of the black soot stained my white shirtsleeves each time I wiped my sweaty brow.

Back then, we could see, smell, even taste the dirty air, but we had no sense of actual pollution levels. Now, our smartphones tell us more than we want to know. I check every day, and every day the numbers are bad.

The worst offender is particulate matter—the schmutz that would still dirty my shirts if I could wear the white long-sleeved tops I brought from home instead of the short-sleeved orange polo shirts our school requires. It's not just an outdoor problem. Though we clean our kitchen table every evening, before breakfast we have to sponge off the fresh layer of soot that finds its way indoors overnight. Keeping the windows shut protects us moderately well from insects, but the seals aren't good enough to keep the air pollution out.

It's small particles, less than two and a half micrometers in diameter, that are the most dangerous, because they go deep into the respiratory system and get stuck there. I'm not an expert, but I do know a thing or two about PM2.5 from my past life in science. My most popular research paper—front-page news across the US in the summer of 2015—showed how airborne PM2.5 spikes the evening of July Fourth, due to that most American of festivities, Independence Day fireworks. "Oh say, can you breathe?" asked the clever headlines. The unprinted answer: "Probably better not."

At home, I had to explain to friends, relatives, and reporters why PM2.5 is a problem and why they might want to watch their hometown fireworks from an upwind location. In Thailand, everyone we encounter knows the dangers of PM2.5, but they seem to take a more accepting, karmic perspective than I can muster.

We have a PM2.5 monitor at school, and every day I force myself to look at it. There is an official definition of "good" air quality, which we've yet to experience in Pathum Thani. Only a few days have crept into the "moderate" zone. Most days the air is "unhealthy" or "unhealthy for sensitive groups." On the worst days, everyone wears a facemask outdoors to filter at least some of the particles. The kids don't mind the masks, which inspire zombie games and riotous laughter. I find them nasty and annoying—collectors of sweat and saliva that fog up my eye-glasses. Getting accustomed to mask-wearing is a valuable lesson, though, and we are lucky to have a stockpile we brought from home in our suitcase of medical supplies. Masks will become a scarce commodity in a few months, when a novel coronavirus takes the place of air pollution as the scariest airborne threat.

All of this is to say that we are tolerating both the air pollution and the idea that breathing in Thailand is probably shaving a few days, or maybe months, off our life expectancy. The air quality index be damned, we are heading to Bangkok for the weekend. After almost a month in our Pathum Thani dorm, we need a break. Our three priorities are basic creature comforts.

We need a good night's sleep. Our bedroom air conditioner is no match for the relentless heat, and our plastic-covered, extra-firm mattress ensures we bathe in sweat every night and wake up with sore backs every morning. A hotel bed, with luxury sheets and extra pillows, would be a dream come true.

We need a long, hot shower. Our semi-outdoor bathroom houses fluctuating populations of ants, mosquitos, and little lizards. We use the showerhead to rinse them off the walls, the toilet, and the urinal before washing ourselves. Then we towel off on the balcony, hoping no one is watching from the field below. Nothing about the arrangement is relaxing.

And we need a rice-free meal. The daily fare for lunch at school is scrambled eggs and steamed rice, which seems to be the Thai equivalent of mac and cheese or PB&J, a meal every kid enjoys. Dinner at the neighborhood food stalls is often *khao pad* (fried rice), a spiced-up version of the same basic ingredients. Something as simple as a crusty loaf of bread would take me a long way toward heaven. A cheese pizza, oh my! The idea of a tangy tomato sauce makes me drool.

Only slightly less essential is Steve's need to catch up on hometown sports. Our habitually heartbreaking Nationals are in their first World Series in eighty-three years, and we have neither a television nor Cracker Jack in Pathum Thani.

There's no yoga studio in Pathum Thani, either. I've been practicing in our apartment, but I haven't taken, or taught, a class since we left the US, and I'm slowly but surely losing strength and flexibility. Visiting the Iyengar yoga studio in Bangkok would be a treat for me, but not for Steve, who insists on referring to himself as a failed yogi. I'll find a hotel with an exercise room and practice there. Though my teacher, Martha, would be disappointed to hear me admit it, getting my butt to the yoga studio isn't my top priority on our first weekend in Bangkok in almost thirty years. Steve and I should do some sightseeing and find out how our honeymoon memories of Bangkok compare with present-day reality.

On the final day of that honeymoon visit, we discovered the Chao Phraya River ferries, offering a cooler, quieter, less frenetic alternative to the city's roadways, as well as cleaner air. Based on intel from a teacher at school, it seems we can get to Bangkok by taking a taxi about ten kilometers to Pak Kret then boarding the Chao Phraya Express for a scenic, half-hour ride downstream to Bangkok's main pier at Sathorn Road. I book a room at the Riverside Hotel, which runs its own ferry from Sathorn, so we can completely avoid the streets of Bangkok.

"Let's go to a temple," I suggest to Steve as we finalize our plans. We visited two iconic riverside temples during that long-ago trip—Wat Pho on the east bank with its enormous golden Reclining Buddha, and Wat Arun, whose position on the opposite shore makes it a glory at dawn.

Steve isn't enthusiastic, even when I suggest we "make

merit"—light incense, give money, and offer garlands of orange marigolds—at one of the temples. I'm not interested in racking up karma credit, but these Buddhist gestures seem a fitting way to show gratitude for having survived our first weeks in Thailand.

"We're going to Bangkok. We should do *something* Thai," I argue. "We can't spend all weekend eating pizza and watching TV in a hotel room."

"I don't see why not," Steve says. "We have dozens of weekends ahead of us, and we can go to Bangkok any time. That's the advantage of living in Pathum Thani." Steve is right. Though we'll spend the occasional weekend in Pathum Thani, and we'll explore a few other Thai towns, Bangkok will become our second home in Thailand. This first trip is an exploratory mission, our chance to get reacquainted with the city.

On Friday catching a cab on the highway outside the school gate is, as always, a snap. Eventually the driver understands our "Pak Kret Chao Phraya" to mean we are going to the ferry pier. Our request is about as specific as saying "Washington Potomac" to a DC taxi driver and hoping to get to the District Wharf, but miraculously it works.

What doesn't work is the ferry to Bangkok. At the pier, there are no signs or ticket offices. An ancient, wooden, open-air boat, with seating for about a dozen, pulls up to the pier. We board along with a handful of other people, and the boat immediately sets sail. And immediately stops, directly on the other side of the river, to let all the passengers, except Steve and me, disembark. It then chugs back to the departure dock, ready to make the five-minute round-trip again.

Back onshore, a young Thai man takes pity on a couple of confused *farangs* and explains that the Pak Kret–Bangkok commuter ferry makes the downstream trip only on weekday

119

mornings—there's no boat to Bangkok on Friday evening. We can take the bus to Victory Monument, transfer to the subway, walk a few blocks, then take a quick ferry to our destination.

"I'm going to Victory Monument," he says. "I'll show you which bus to take and where to get off." He seems completely trustworthy and, like so many Thais we've encountered, genuinely interested in helping.

The bus is old and, even with the windows open, it's stuffy, but it's a comfortable enough trip, and the MRT station is right by the bus stop. Bangkok has two rail systems: the underground Mass Rapid Transit and the elevated Skytrain, both new since our last visit. The MRT station is clean, spacious, and easy to navigate with helpful uniformed attendants everywhere. Trains run frequently and smoothly. Passengers queue up politely when boarding and follow posted instructions to give priority seating to disabled, elderly, and pregnant passengers and to monks. Two teenage girls in school uniforms offer Steve and me their seats as soon as we board our train, proving the practical value of a head of gray hair in cultures where age confers respect. Unlike Washington's Metrorail system, where even locals can't understand the garbled announcements of complicated station names, here stops are broadcast in beautifully enunciated Thai and English. Visitors have to try hard to get lost on Bangkok's rail system.

"It's not the ferry, but it's pretty cool!" I say to Steve.

"Yup, it's fast and the AC is great, if that's what you mean," he replies. Underground, indoors, and air-conditioned, the MRT air quality is at least one, maybe two categories better than today's "unhealthy" rating outdoors.

From the subway, it's a short walk to Sathorn Pier where we find our hotel ferry, with a prominent sign in English, for a five-minute ride downstream. Even in the dark, it's clear this isn't the sleepy shoreline we remember. Steel-and-glass shopping centers and towering hotels light up the sky, testament to Bangkok's phenomenal growth and modernization. What was in 1990 a city of six million souls now is home to almost twice as many. The skyline, then distinguished by highly ornamented, steeply pitched traditional Thai rooflines, is now dominated by skyscrapers.

One of these high-rises is the Riverside, where I fall in love at first sight. Each member of the staff greets us with a sparkling smile and *wai*. On bended knee, a slender woman offers an enchanting purple tea made from butterfly pea flowers that is just sweet enough to revive us after our introduction to so many of Bangkok's public transportation options.

Our room has the promised river view plus an unexpected bonus—a Jacuzzi bath. After a quick rinse in the shower, I soak for so long that I almost fall asleep in the tub. Cleaner than I've been in weeks and swaddled in a terry-cloth robe, I emerge from the bathroom to find Steve channel-surfing our huge wall-mounted television.

"Any luck?" I ask, knowing that he's looking for a network that broadcasts American sports.

"We can watch a cricket tournament, or auto racing, or any number of soccer games, in about a dozen different languages, but no baseball," Steve says in frustration.

"It's nine in the morning at home. We'll try tomorrow. Maybe they'll broadcast the game live. But now, this gorgeous bed beckons." We retire to the clean, fresh linens, sigh, and sleep till the golden dawn.

At daybreak, we are the only swimmers in the most glorious pool I've ever seen. Instead of Pee Wee's broom sweeping the pavement at school, we hear boats starting to move along the river and Bangkok waking to the new day.

The capital has changed since our honeymoon, and so have our needs. Without even raising the subject, we both know that this will not be our last weekend in Bangkok.

At breakfast, the assortment of people around the room makes me realize how much I have missed life in a cosmopolitan city. There is a large contingent of northern Europeans, whose bulk makes the Thai staff look waiflike, and several tables of Muslims, each with a single man in Western attire accompanied by three or four black-clad women in a variety of head coverings, from colorful silk scarves to full niqab. There are Asian parents and grandparents, hand-feeding their children, and a smattering of Americans.

But it's the buffet that really gets my attention. It seems endless and offers something to remind everyone of home. One counter features mezze and pita, another is an omelet station with cases of European cheeses, breads, and pastries nearby. There are Japanese, Korean, and Chinese dishes, as well as *tom yum goong* and other Thai specialties. It is hard to focus and make selections, though we have no trouble foregoing the rice-forward Asian offerings.

An hour later, having sampled the cuisine of at least four continents, we refill our coffee cups to rest and reconnoiter the room. At a table across from the pancake station are four Americans in T-shirts and ball caps, the only people in the room wearing head coverings other than the Muslim ladies. I find my too-casual compatriots a bit embarrassing, but Steve wants a little connection with home and goes over to say hello.

Within moments, they are engaged in animated conversation and have attracted the attention of the quiet black-clad women and a noodle-slurping Japanese couple at neighboring tables. Avoiding the commotion, I turn my attention to a lovely slice of pale green pandan sponge cake, only to be disturbed by a huge cheer from the Americans.

"New friends?" I ask Steve when he finally returns to our table.

"Heck no, they're Astros fans." The five-pointed Texas stars on their caps somehow didn't register with me earlier. The Astros, down two games to one, have just scored a run in the Friday night game at Nationals Park. "I wished them good luck," Steve says, as he takes out his smartphone to find the live broadcast.

At the Thai section of the buffet, I fill a bowl with peanuts. "What, no Cracker Jack?" Steve asks, as we settle in for the final innings. Merit-making can wait until afternoon. And until I've double-checked the ferry schedule.

Orchids on the Water

Khru Nok will countenance no wallflowers.

Bowls and baskets overflowing with orange marigolds, purple orchids, and white chrysanthemums cover the floor. Their fragrances fill the classroom. Tomorrow is the full moon of the twelfth month of the Thai lunar calendar. To prepare for the Loy Krathong celebration, Khru Nok is teaching our students how to make floating baskets.

The moment she speaks those two Thai words, a fragment of melody from long ago invades my head. In October 1990, Steve and I heard it everywhere—in our Bangkok hotel lobby, in Chiang Mai's marketplaces, at the beach in Hua Hin. The refrain *"loy, loy krathong"* was the soundtrack to our honeymoon. Twenty-nine years later, I still regret our ill-informed itinerary. We left Thailand before the full moon, so our only experience of the holiday was this earworm. Now, in Pathum Thani, we are getting a second chance.

Twice a week we happily hand the class over to Khru Nok, who teaches our Thai students their mother tongue. But today Khru Nok insists we join her lesson. After all, she says, everyone needs a *krathong* to honor the water goddess Phra Mae Khongkha, cast off bad karma, and welcome what Thai people call the cold season.

Two parts of the banana tree are essential for crafting a

krathong. She gives us each an enormous leaf and a saucer-sized slice of stem. With blunt-nosed scissors designed for tiny hands, we cut our leaves into circles and strips, then fold the strips into perky cat-ear triangles. We use straight pins to cover the pithy stems with the shiny green circles and to rim the circumference with the triangles to create a basket. With a basin of water, Khru Nok shows us how our *krathongs*, which resemble little lily pads, float equally well.

Next we fill our baskets with flowers. Some children make riotous piles of color. Others create meticulously symmetrical arrangements. Unsure of Thai design sensibility, I keep mine minimalist—orchids only. As we work on our baskets, I suddenly hear the melody. It isn't exactly my earworm—memory must have modulated the original into a Westernized version—but it's surely the Loy Krathong song.

Most of the children know the lyrics and are singing along. A few of the K2s spontaneously form a line to promenade around the classroom, their arms swaying rhythmically overhead. Khru Nok rearranges the children, pairing each pro with a novice or two, and soon everyone has the steps of the simple dance.

Everyone except Steve and me. We don't dance much, and when we do it's more of a freeform affair. But Khru Nok's special smile of encouragement is irresistible. After tucking orchids behind our ears, she has us literally follow in her footsteps around the room until we absorb the rudiments of what I now gather is an essential element of the holiday.

We all need to work on the graceful hand gestures that make this dance truly Thai. Khru Nok's long fingers arch like swallows' wings. I'm convinced that every elegant movement has meaning, though exactly what remains a mystery. With each circuit around the room and each repetition of the song, my steps grow lighter until, magically, I no longer have to think. Everyone is moving in synchrony. We are floating.

Steve and I head to school the next morning eager to experience the holiday. We march with our class to the *rong rian* sports field to join the rest of the school for the festivities. Everyone is resplendent in traditional Thai attire. The children wear silk bloomer pants in dazzling colors, highlighted with golden threads that shimmer in the sunlight. The girls are in frilly tops, the boys in white jackets with gold buttons. Teachers wear styles ranging from Hmong tribal garb with colorful embroidery to southern Thai fisherman pants with patchwork pockets. Khru Nok looks elegant in a purple sarong skirt and gold silk brocade jacket. Steve and I are self-conscious, and underdressed, in our American attire.

The crowd quiets down as Dr. Pat steps onto a platform and begins her welcome address, not a word of which I understand until she utters, *"Amerigaa."* I wonder what possible link she could make between this uniquely Thai holiday and the United States. A moment later, she is looking straight at Steve and me, gesturing for us to join her onstage.

Making our way across the field, I frantically try to formulate remarks suitable to the occasion. The panic on Steve's face tells me he is doing the same, but we have no time to compare notes.

When we reach the platform, the music begins. *Loy, loy krathong.* No speeches are required. It's worse. Dr. Pat beckons us to follow her as she dances down the running track. Her steps are graceful and intricate. And completely unfamiliar. Apparently, what we learned in the classroom yesterday was the kindergarten version, but suddenly even that vanishes.

Steve and I scan the assembly for Khru Nok, but she is lost in the crowd.

All eyes on us, we have no choice but to follow Dr. Pat as she leads the procession. Arms doing a hula wave, I improvise a step-together-step. Steve hisses, "We never signed up for this," then reluctantly tries to follow my lead.

The oldest students first, class after class joins the parade as the song plays over and over again. Rounding the second bend, I spot Khru Nok with our class. Seeing them, I want to disappear.

But Steve laughs aloud. Our kids, unfazed by our mangled steps, join his laughter and applaud. They are laughing with us, not at us, and suddenly I can't imagine them doing otherwise. Inspired by Khru Nok's example, they press their palms and bow their heads toward us to *wai*, and now it's their turn to enter the dance. By the time we complete the initial lap, we are going with the flow, buoyed by the crowd.

When the music stops, Dr. Pat signals the highlight of the ceremony—the launching of our hundreds of *krathongs* into a body of water. Once more, and equally unexpectedly, she invites Steve and me, as honored guests, to set our *krathong* afloat first.

This isn't the enchanting, moonlit scene that I imagine will unfold tonight across the kingdom: candle-lit *krathongs* drifting on Bangkok's canals, along Chiang Mai's Ping River, and on the beaches rimming the Gulf of Thailand.

It's better. With a nod to Khru Nok and another to Steve, I lower my *krathong* of white orchids into an improvised inflatable splash pool. A gentle push sends it floating toward the other baskets gradually covering the water's surface. With an exhalation and a little prayer, I release my American anxieties to the water goddess.

Lizards at Lumphini

In conversations over the past two months, it's become clear that our kindergartners are obsessed with two species of animal: Thai water buffalo and unicorns. Neither Steve nor I have yet to see a specimen of either in Pathum Thani, and apart from us, Americans are equally rare in these parts. We have never felt any form of anti-American discrimination or discourtesy. On the contrary, our nationality, or perhaps our age, seems to confer some social standing. But our age and nationality do set us apart from the other teachers at school, and sometimes we feel like a pair of lumbering old water buffalo surrounded by lovely young unicorns.

So we are delighted to connect with Saul, Steve's former colleague from their days at the White House, who suggests a get-together in Bangkok. Saul, who was once part of the itinerant community of international bureaucrats, is now settled, married, and raising a family in Thailand. He has invited us to a Sunday morning gathering for American expats. If we're very lucky, Steve says, we might even score an invitation to an expat Thanksgiving dinner next week.

Would that be lucky, actually? If we can't spend the holiday the way we do every year, at my sister Nancy's house, maybe we shouldn't bother. One year we skipped the trip to Massachusetts. The whole family had been with us in Maryland the weekend before Thanksgiving to celebrate Rose's bat mitzvah, and we decided to have the holiday dinner in a restaurant, just the three of us. A French restaurant.

I hadn't appreciated the extent to which Rose associated Thanksgiving with a plate piled high with mashed potatoes made with plenty of butter and cream (not milk, heaven forbid), Aunt Nancy style. *Pommes dauphinoise* wouldn't cut it, nor could pumpkin crème brûlée hold a candle to Nancy's pumpkin (and apple and pecan) pies. That dinner was a big faux pas, one Rose would not soon let me forget. Thanksgiving is the ultimate family festival. Do we really want to spend the day with a bunch of strangers just because they're American?

These won't be just any old Americans, however. They are members of Democrats Abroad Thailand, and the event, snarkily billed "Walk with the Lizards in Lumphini to Expel the Ones in DC," is a fundraiser.

Steve has been suffering withdrawal from the worlds of sports and politics and is keen to connect with Saul and his friends. I'm curious about the monitor lizards.

The geography lesson in our orientation to Thailand included a segment on Thai wildlife, with a predictable focus on what animal rights advocates call "charismatic megafauna"— endangered and exploited elephants, tigers, and primates—and on feral dogs, which we were simultaneously warned to avoid as potential rabies carriers and encouraged to help by donating to, or volunteering with, canine rescue organizations.

We were warned about monitor lizards, too. They are so reviled here that their Thai name is a grave insult never to be uttered aloud. The Democrats can't resist the metaphor.

We arrive early at the King Rama VI statue on Rama IV Road in Lumphini Park, a refreshing expanse of green in the city dense with skyscrapers. Thai kings for more than two centuries have taken the name Rama, the hero of Thailand's national story, the Ramakien, and an ancestor of the Buddha.

"You found us!" calls Saul from across the plaza. He and Steve share a warm embrace and exchange generous, if untrue, compliments on how neither has changed a bit in the decade since they were last together. He introduces us to his young son John and the rest of the group, including several parents with kids in tow.

Our nature guide is another expat American. A professional herpetologist, he is decked out in khaki safari hat, photographer's vest, and chukka boots, with binoculars and a fancy camera hanging from his neck. The rest of us, dressed for a morning stroll in a well-manicured urban park and lunch in a downtown restaurant, follow him toward the pond in search of lizards. Steve and I walk with Saul, John, a woman from the US Embassy, and a Bangkok-based journalist. Predictably, the conversation is all about preparations for the 2020 presidential elections. His long deprivation over, Steve is back in his element, talking politics, public policy, and polls.

But the US primaries won't begin for months, and *not* talking politics since we left home has been a welcome respite for me, so I jog ahead to join the guide. Before I can say hello, he shushes me and puts his binoculars up to his face.

"Pied fantail," he whispers, pointing to a nearby tree.

I look but see no birds. "Guess I missed it."

He stays quiet, binoculars in place, apparently less interested in me than in more clever creatures. I walk on.

As I approach a long pond, they suddenly come into view. Five monitor lizards bask, unperturbed and still as statues, except for an occasional slow turn of a head. Their inertia seems prehistoric, surreal, and out of sync with bustling Bangkok just outside Lumphini. Then one lizard drags its meter-long tail through the grass and slips into the water. I continue down the path to join a cluster of children and parents at the water's edge. One girl is peering through a pair of child-sized red binoculars.

"Excited to see the lizards?" I ask her.

"Ac-tu-al-ly," she replies, distinctly pronouncing all four syllables, "I prefer the turtles."

I'm instantly charmed. When Rose was a little girl, her diction was just like this child's.

"Oh, why?" I ask.

"Well," she considers, drawing out the word as she lowers her binoculars, "it's cool how they sometimes suck in their legs and all you can see is their shells."

"And what do they do in there?"

She considers a moment. "Well, I think maybe they meditate."

"Like the Buddha?"

"Like me. At school," explains my precocious new friend.

And then I start to hum the gentle Thai melody we sing in kindergarten every morning. She knows the English lyrics. *I'm breathing in. I'm breathing out. As flowers bloom.*

Together, in whispers, we finish the song, with our matching hand gestures for each line. *The mountains high. The rivers sigh. The air that I breathe. I fly.* Her face is tranquil, like our students' when we finish this daily ritual.

"I see you have your own private nature guide," Steve says as he approaches. "Did you get a good look at the monitor lizards?"

"Ob-vi-ous-ly," my companion answers. "They're everywhere. Did *you* see the *turtles?*"

"Nope, I did not," says Steve. "Guess my eyes aren't as sharp as yours." His you're-cute-as-a-button-but-I'm-taking-you-seri-ously tone tells me he too can hear echoes of Rose in this girl's voice.

She seizes the opportunity to show off her nifty binoculars but struggles to adjust them for Steve's grown-up-sized face.

"Wait here. I'll be right back." She finds the herpetologist and, as she tugs on his vest with an entitled familiarity, I'm con-vinced she says, "Daddy, can I borrow your binocs?" I'm hoping he won't spoil our meeting by accompanying her back to us, and I realize I'm becoming a bona fide introvert kindergarten teacher—the type of adult who would rather sing a song, read a book, or watch turtles with a child than talk politics, or business, or even pied fantails with an adult.

As we walk toward the subway to begin our journey back to Pathum Thani, I ask Steve, "Did you have fun?"

"I'll say! This is a really savvy group. But unfortunately no mention of Thanksgiving. I guess we'll be having pad thai and *som tum* in Pathum Thani."

"That's fine by me," I answer truthfully. I wonder whether the curriculum at Pathum Thani Prep could accommodate a les-son on Thanksgiving. And whether our kids might like to try mashed potatoes.

Cornucopia

The following weekend we are back in Bangkok and on a mission. We need storybooks, particularly books about Thanksgiving, which is fast approaching. First, we try a huge chain bookseller in one of Bangkok's luxury malls. Like Barnes & Noble in its heyday, the store has eye-catching displays of merchandise—puzzles, stationery, mugs, knickknacks and, yes, some books. We scour the shelves for children's classics but find only spinoffs from kiddie TV shows and workbooks promising to transform every child, your child, into a little Einstein.

A friendly clerk suggests we try a secondhand bookshop on Sukhumvit Road, the main commercial boulevard running through downtown Bangkok and continuing five hundred kilometers all the way to the Cambodian border. If we can't find what we want on Sukhumvit, we won't find it anywhere.

I am a big fan of picture books. Those little gems of literature are lifelines in the classroom when carefully planned lessons go awry or finish too early. But our school, which is fully equipped with art supplies, toys, and Montessori materials, is surprisingly short on books. We've already read and reread most of our classroom library, and we need more.

"We must have passed it," I tell Steve. "Let's double back."

Sure enough, we walked right past the narrow storefront with haphazard stacks of books in the window. The white-and-gray sign seems expressly designed *not* to attract attention. Even before we open the door and the brass shopkeeper's bell announces our presence, my brain conjures the special secondhand bookshop blend of scents that awaits us—must, dust, glue, and for reasons I've never understood, vanilla.

Unlike the glitzy mall store with its steel display cases and fluorescent lights, this place is a paean to forest products—walls lined with wooden shelves, well-worn hardwood floors, wood-beamed ceilings, and books jammed into every niche. A book on student political movements in Thailand immediately catches Steve's eye. I am distracted by a shelf of Thai authors in English translation. I sit for a bit with M. R. Kukrit Pramoj's 1954 collection *Many Lives* (translated in 1996 by Meredith Borthwick) in which a passenger boat on the Chao Phraya River is lost in a storm. Each poignant story tells of one of the many lives that perish and reveals a glimpse of Thai society and culture.

The story titles are the simple, one- or two-syllable names of each main character. They remind me of our students' cute Thai nicknames. Which reminds me of the actual purpose of this shopping trip. Having hardly ventured past the entrance, I get up out of my squat and approach the three clerks perched on wooden stools, busily scrutinizing a box of used books from a potential seller.

A young woman with black-framed glasses and pigtails sprouting from the top of her head escorts me up the steep staircase to the children's section. Her English has a vaguely British inflection, but she knows about Thanksgiving and shows me several shelves of holiday books for kids. I make a quick perusal then carefully descend the steps to find Steve.

"We may be in luck," I tell Steve, who has moved from politics to mysteries, "but you've got to come help. Otherwise, I'll be here until closing."

We spend the next hour sorting through stacks and stacks of picture books, pausing to read aloud pages of special treasures— *Jamberry*, which our daughter adored, *Make Way for Ducklings*, which my father, a Boston native with the accent to prove it, used to read to me a half century ago. We add these to the growing stack of keepers. Then Steve finds a shelf-full of Christmas stories and announces, "I think we're getting close."

We rummage through books on Halloween, Hanukkah, Diwali, and even Anzac Day before Steve finally holds up *Thanks for Thanksgiving*.

"Oh, thank goodness," I say. "Any more?" I'm planning to bypass the curriculum, which calls for a weeklong focus on water transportation. Instead, our reading theme will be Thanksgiving, and I'll need as many stories as we can muster. We find two more then start building another pile for after the holiday.

After reluctantly jettisoning what we can't squeeze into our backpack, we head downstairs to pay. We've spent a bit more than we had planned—book shopping is ever thus—but we've just bought ourselves, and our kids, hours of kindergarten joy.

"Come again," says the pigtailed clerk.

"Without a doubt," I reply.

•••

On Monday Steve reads *Jamberry* to the class but only makes it partway through the book, because the children have so much to say about the jam-packed illustrations. They will finish the story on Tuesday and, by popular demand, reread it on Wednesday.

Thursday morning, in the school kitchen, I put on an apron. I feel like an impostor. A world away, in Massachusetts, my sister is assuredly in her special red-and-white-checked pie-baking apron. But I have work to do. Part of our job, as I see it, is to introduce the kids to American culture. My lesson objectives for today are delicious and ambitious: students will be able to bake pumpkin pie and articulate gratitude.

After passing around the cinnamon and vanilla for sniff tests, and under close supervision, the children take turns whisking together the eggs, evaporated milk, and mashed pumpkin and miraculously manage to keep most of the mixture in the bowl. Everyone presses balls of dough into muffin tins, then carefully ladles in the filling. While our pies bake, we read *Happy Thanksgiving, Biscuit.*

Afraid to deviate too much from the standard menu, I stick with scrambled eggs, steamed rice, and chicken stir-fry for our Thanksgiving lunch. But our holiday dessert is a hit with the kids and teachers alike, in no small part because of the whipped cream Steve squirts on each miniature pumpkin pie and on each extended index finger.

Before we head back to the classroom, I try one more holiday tradition. "In America," I begin, "at our family's Thanksgiving dinner, we go around the table, and every person says what they are most thankful for. Shall we try that today?"

I ask Steve to go first, to model the exercise. "I'm thankful for pumpkin pie!" he announces. As he certainly expects, I roll my eyes.

While he hasn't done much to appeal to our better angels, he has gotten the ball rolling, and a moment later Ivy pipes in, "Me too. I'm thankful for pumpkin pie. And whipped cream."

Continuing our food theme, Lek offers, "I'm thankful for strawberry jam," and Chompoo pipes up with, "and blueberry... on toast bread." I can't help but smile. Until today's pie party, putting the kitchen's never-before-used toaster into action has been my only successful innovation to our lunchtime repertoire.

Sai announces that she is thankful for unicorns, and the class erupts in laughter. Athit can't, or won't, contribute to the conversation, and I don't force the issue. Next is Chet, who says, "I'm thankful for *Jamberry*." Then, "And I'm thankful for Teacher Dian."

From the look on my face, the rest of the kids know exactly what to say next. There's a chorus of "I'm thankful for Teacher Dian," and "I'm thankful for Teacher Steve," and "I'm thankful for Teacher Candace," and "I'm thankful for Teacher Miranda." Everyone, even Athit, is laughing, and all four teachers are wiping away tears.

Miranda asks, "And Teacher Dian, what are *you* thankful for?"

No response other than "I'm thankful for all of you" is even remotely possible. And today it's true.

Beloved Voices

Getting Thai mobile phone accounts was a top priority when we arrived in Chiang Mai. They've been our lifeline, but much more for the data plan than for voice. No one in Thailand phones us, relying instead on social media messaging. Because of the time difference, all our communication with folks back home is by email. So far, our only calls have been with the phone company, in an ongoing—and so far fruitless—effort to pay our bill.

Rather than lots of personal messages, I'm sending periodic *Missives from Thailand* to a list of friends and family and enjoying the replies that trickle in over the following days. It's a bit like the other time I lived abroad, a miserable year in Belgium as a graduate student, when international phone calls were beyond my budget and letters on pale blue airmail paper were bright spots in otherwise damp, dreary, and often dark days.

All of which is to say that this morning's Skype call is a very special event. My whole side of the family, gathered in Massachusetts for Thanksgiving, is taking a breather between dinner and dessert.

Massachusetts: Happy Thanksgiving! Hi, Aunt Dian! Hi, Uncle Steve! Oh, sweetheart.
Pathum Thani: Look at you all! Oh wow!

Look at them all, squeezing together, trying to fit in the frame. All those dear faces. Mom looks good, thank God. Cousin Lizzie, too.

Oh my gosh! Rose brought Elliot. She looks good. Really happy. Him too. Bringing the boyfriend to meet the grand-mother—this is a Big Deal.

Massachusetts: How *are* you? You've lost weight. How's Thailand? Is that your apartment? You both look great.
Pathum Thani: Hold on! One at a time, okay?

They look great. Grinning and waving like crazy people at a baseball game who suddenly see themselves on the big screen over center field.

Can Mom actually tell that we've lost weight? She always says that when we visit. Just a few pounds for me, but Steve's really melting away.

Pathum Thani: We're fine. Everything's good. But we want to hear all about your dinner!
Massachusetts: Aunt Nancy outdid herself. Homemade corn-bread. Kale with cranberries. Mashed potatoes, of course. Stuffing, inside and outside the turkey, of course. Look, three different pies.
Pathum Thani: I'm drooling. Is that a cake, too?
Massachusetts: For Rose's birthday.

An aunt for the ages, she is. Thank you, sis.

Massachusetts: How about you? Have you eaten yet?
Pathum Thani: We just had breakfast. School starts in an hour.

Massachusetts: Oh, right. So what are you planning for dinner? Or was Thanksgiving yesterday? Are you ahead or behind?

Pathum Thani: Yesterday. We made mini pumpkin pies. A little baking class for the kids.

Massachusetts: What else?

Pathum Thani: Oh, the usual. Scrambled eggs and steamed rice.

Massachusetts: Oh, no. For Thanksgiving! You're making me cry.

Pathum Thani: No, don't. It was fine, really. Aww . . . Mom, how are you feeling?

Her face looks odd. Is she having a stroke or something? Oh God.

Pathum Thani: Mom, are you okay? Nancy, what's going on?

Massachusetts: Give her a minute. She's just a bit overwhelmed.

Massachusetts: No, no. I'm all right. Oh, I'm sorry. I love your letters, but it's so good to see your faces.

Thank God.

Pathum Thani: Yours too, Mom.

Massachusetts: Did you do the *What are you thankful for?* ritual with your kiddos?

Pathum Thani: Of course! Don't tell me you didn't.

Massachusetts: Er…we're saving that for dessert.

Hmmph. When the cat's away…

Pathum Thani: Mom, sorry, what did you say?

Massachusetts: I said I'll be thankful when you two are home safe and sound.

Is this Jewish mother guilt-tripping? That's not like her. Or
is she really worried? For us, or for herself?

Pathum Thani: We'll be home for Passover, okay? We'll talk again
before then, though. All right? Soon.
Massachusetts: Sure. Of course. I'll make pumpkin pie.
Pathum Thani: For Passover?
Massachusetts: Oops. We'll figure it out. Love you. Be safe. Take
care of each other.

Of course, we'll take care of each other. And so will they.
What am I thankful for? For all of them.

Buoyant Memory

You kick, and then you glide
You kick, and then you glide
Keep breathing, it's the most important part
It's all in the rhythm of the heart

When I swim breaststroke, I often sing these lyrics in my head. I've sung them since the late seventies, when I first heard them on *Music from the Hearts of Space*, a program I taped, probably illegally, from KPFA, the lefty, folk-y, New Age-y Berkeley radio station that was the soundtrack of my college years. My Memorex tape got tangled long ago, and I haven't heard the tune since, but I know Nina Wise's *The Swim Song* by heart.

This morning, the melody in my head is just one strain of the Pathum Thani soundscape. Bird songs, more full-throated than our Maryland varieties, blend with the rumble of highway traffic and the soft slap-slap of Steve's arms hitting the water in the lane next to mine. I pause to remove my goggles for my final laps, always backstroke, and to witness the rim of sun creeping over the horizon, tingeing the whole hazy dome of sky sherbet pink.

Piercing this morning chorus, the childlike voice calling, "Good morning, Teacher Dian," couldn't startle me more. The figure waving from the pool deck is clad in black from neck to wrists and ankles, gigantic black goggles dominating the round face. I almost mistake the tiny body for a student's. Then I recognize the smile as Laoshi Ling's.

"You're here!" I shout. For weeks, the young Chinese teacher has been promising to join Steve and me for a morning swim. But each time I've reminded her, she's apologized, claiming she couldn't drag herself out of bed so early. Ling's workday is several hours longer than ours, but I've tried to convince her that swimming at daybreak will boost her energy and her spirits.

"Jump in," I say, "the water's gorgeous." Ling hesitates then walks to the ladder and holds the rail as she skims her toes through the water.

By now, Steve has noticed we have company and interrupts his laps to call out, "Come on in, the water's great!"

Ling waves and looks at the water.

"It's not cold," I say. Nothing is ever cold in Pathum Thani. But Ling's problem isn't the temperature.

"I'm frightened," she says, and even through her humungous goggles I can see she's not joking. When she told me she had wanted to join the after-school Swim Academy, I assumed she was an experienced swimmer looking for a coached workout. No, she wanted lessons. Unfortunately, Swim Academy is just for kids.

Fear not, Laoshi Ling! Teacher Dian to the rescue! I duck under the lane divider, swim to the corner, pat the concrete edge of the pool, and tell Ling to sit.

"Just get your feet wet, okay?" I say, and she complies.

I'm reminded of the last time I faced a girl sitting at the edge of a pool, more than twenty-five years ago. Our daughter was still a baby. At her first swim lessons, I'd hold out my arms, and Steve, on the deck with her, would guide her into the water and my embrace.

I hold out my arms to Ling and say, "I'm right here," just as I must have said to Rose years ago. Ling puts her hands in mine, then slowly slides them up to my shoulders as she eases her way into the water. She laughs nervously, trying to stay steady, as I keep my eyes fixed on her foggy goggles.

Steve moves into our lane and tilts his chin toward the clock outside the coach's office. It's almost 6:30. We all need to shower, eat, and be at school by 7:30. But I want Ling to do more than simply stand in the water.

"Want to float?" I ask her. After a moment's hesitation Ling lets go of the ladder.

She's too nervous to lie back, so I slide my arms under her, just as I did with Rose. Buoyed by the water and supported by my arms, Ling's face and whole body seem to relax. A good place to end our first lesson.

As we cross the *soi* between the pool and the dorms, I suggest a second lesson tomorrow morning, but Ling has bus duty.

"Next week, then," I tell her.

"I'm going to teach that girl to swim," I say to Steve over breakfast. "Just like I taught Rose."

"Just like *who* taught Rose?" he says.

"Me," I say.

"No," he says. "Don't you remember? She always wanted *me* in the pool for those kiddy lessons."

I stop chewing. Can he be right?

Steve taught Rose to ride a bike. I'm sure of that. He's a runner, and there's no question which parent would have trotted alongside as Rose learned to pedal and balance. But I'm the more devoted swimmer and have long believed swimming to be the ideal lifetime sport. I'd have wanted to teach my only child to swim.

"I'm positive," he says. "There's that photo. It used to be in her bathroom. In a tiny frame decorated with fish. Remember?"

And then I do remember. Before Rose was born, I painted the bathroom high-gloss turquoise and bought a tropical fish shower curtain. Fish-themed yard sale finds, like that little frame with corals and clownfish, came later. I remember snipping the picture to fit.

I must have taken the photo of Steve and Rose in the pool together. Yet in my memory, in my body even, I'm sharing my love of the water with my daughter, holding her afloat.

Her mother taught her how to swim
When she was very, very young
And swimming to survive
And swimming to survive

That's how *The Swim Song* begins. I've always told people that my mother, who was a graceful, Esther Williams–style swimmer, taught me how to swim when I was very, very young. My father taught me to ride a bike, but my mother loved swimming, and she taught me to love it, too. Didn't she?

When I ask her, my mother tells me I had swimming lessons at the local YMCA. That's odd, because we weren't Y members. Our family belonged to the Jewish Community Center, and now I remember taking lessons there and scraping my nose on the chalk-colored concrete pool edge we used to hold on to while practicing our flutter kick. I can't even picture the Y pool, only the entrance of the big brick building on Pleasant Street that is no more.

My memories are like my body afloat, adjusting to every breeze, ripple, and wave, every breath, thought, and emotion. How did I invent memories of my mother teaching me to swim and of me teaching my own daughter? Do I harbor some deep desire for these particular, aquatic, maternal connections? Or was it the result of repeating *The Swim Song* so many times over so many years?

I hope Rose remembers her first swim lessons more accurately. Her dad was with her in the water. I was there on the sidelines, taking pictures, making memories. Then making them up.

A Party in Pattaya

Despite the dinner crowd on the lantern-lit terrace, it's remarkably quiet. No boozy parties on the pleasure boats anchored in the harbor, no clanking of fittings against masts, not even the lapping of waves on the shore. An eyelash of moonlight is chasing the sun setting into the Gulf of Thailand. This will surely be the darkest, and so the loveliest, Thai sky we've seen. In the cities we've visited—Bangkok, Chiang Mai, and even the outskirts of Pathum Thani—there's a constant hum of traffic, and a haze of humid pollution gives the night a dull but persistent glow. Though they won't last the evening, I'll long remember this hush and this clear sky.

"I hope you like explosions!" says the General with a twinkle in his eyes and a leftward lift of his chin. He and Dr. Pat have invited Steve and me to the coastal resort of Pattaya for the weekend. I'm guessing the General is talking about the *tom yum*, whose chili-rich aromas are wafting over from the next table at this waterside dinner buffet, our first meal together.

"Americans love explosions," Dr. Pat tells him, and I wonder how I'll politely avoid the *tom yum*, a fiery bouillabaisse-like dish that tempted me once and will be seared forever in my memory and my gut. Then she says to Steve and me, "When I was a student in Indiana, I remember the Independence Day explosions. So beautiful." Apparently, the highlight of our evening will be the Pattaya International Fireworks Competition.

I'm one of those people, those party poopers, who don't care for fireworks. The blasts that resonate in my chest, the booms that leave my ears ringing, and the toxic ash in the air are more assault than entertainment. I'll be cringing inwardly when the display begins, though I'll try to ooh and aah in appreciation.

"Come, we'll fill our plates," says Dr. Pat. "Then we'll talk."

"But first, a toast to our guests!" says the General, raising his water glass. That first day in Pathum Thani, and each time we've seen him since, he has insisted on giving us several two-liter bottles of water. "Don't let yourselves get dehydrated," he always instructs us. He is a sweet man, and it's heartwarming to know that someone in Thailand is concerned for our welfare.

"And to our hosts!" Steve counters. "And to a spectacular evening." Steve, who is a sweet man, too, is fond of the General. And of fireworks. His oohs and aahs will be genuine.

At the buffet, Dr. Pat introduces me to one of the chefs as "my American friend." In truth, we hardly know each other— the three-hour drive from Pathum Thani was more time together than we've had in the two months since we met—yet her words plant a signpost at an empty spot inside me that I haven't noticed until now.

I'm not lonely here in Thailand. There isn't time to be lonely at school, and I'm always with Steve the rest of the day. Would I like a Thai friend? Yes, I would. But what does "my American friend" mean? Is it simply easier than introducing me as "my American employee"?

She also introduces me to the chef's *hoi tod*, an oyster omelet, more oyster than egg, crisp-fried in oil and served over crunchy bean sprouts. The chef, familiar with American palates, considerately serves the chili sauce on the side. We'll sample a dozen other specialties tonight, but this is the dish I'll remember with relish.

During the drive from Pathum Thani, we learned that the General served in the Royal Thai Army, that he had occasional connections with US Army counterparts, and that he continues to work in retirement as a military advisor. The General must have been starting his career during the Vietnam War, when the US was operating out of Thai bases and Pattaya was turning from a sleepy fishing village into an R&R destination for American GIs. At sixty-eight, he is one year older than Steve, whose answer to the General's question about whether he served in the war is the truth, if not the whole truth. The draft ended a few months before Steve would have been called up. He doesn't mention his antiwar protests—*Hell No, We Won't Go*—nor do I. Though they may have had little in common as young men, now, as still-working retirees, they seem to share some perspectives on life.

Dr. Pat was less chatty during the trip. While the General drove, she busied herself with her phone.

"So many messages—from the principals, the parents, the government. It never ends, not even on weekends," she apologized. As director of four schools in four Thai provinces, her attention is often elsewhere. Yet she never seems frazzled. This evening, as always, she is composed and gorgeous. Her hair and makeup are perfect, and her designer outfit—wide-legged silk pants, sleeveless top with multicolored sequins, and coordinating beaded kitten-heel sandals—glitters in the candlelight. I'm in functional footwear and my one dress, the one I wore for Loy Krathong. A simple cotton knit, comfortable, wash-and-wear, and decidedly nondescript.

"How did you decide to come to Thailand? Will you retire

here?" the General asks.

Distracted by her phone during dinner, Dr. Pat allowed the three of us to make small talk. Now she silences it and looks at Steve and me. "You're so young," she says, clearly as an extension of her husband's question.

"You're right," Steve says. "We did retire young, in our fifties."

"But," I add, "after leaving government, Steve worked ten more years before retiring again. And for the past few years we've both been volunteer English teachers." I always feel guilty, even on Steve's behalf, about retiring at an age when most people are working, and I feel compelled to justify our choices.

I left science because the arc of my research career had reached a natural conclusion. In the 1980s, when I started in the field, climate scientists had long been predicting that increasing atmospheric carbon dioxide would lead to global warming, sea-level rise, and a host of other changes. But at that time, there was little to no evidence that any of these things were actually happening. Thirty years later, the evidence of climate change was abundant and well established. I had helped establish it, and I was ready to let a new generation build on those contributions and to follow science from the sidelines.

The General tells Steve and me, "You found a good balance. You work, but you have less responsibility. Less stress." He is looking at us, but I suspect he is speaking to his wife and hoping our paths, which seem to parallel his own, will inspire her to join him in retirement, or at least to slow down a bit. Dr. Pat smiles at her husband, but she doesn't take the bait.

"You both are dedicated people," Dr. Pat says. "So is my husband. But you worked for enormous organizations. When you retired, the government went on without you. It's different when you are in charge of everything." I'm positive they've had this conversation before.

I'm on the General's side here. Dr. Pat is constantly traveling. We rarely see her, though there's only a road and a rice field between Pathum Thani Prep and the compound where she and the General live.

"My schools are my life, like my children," she insists. But she knows the score. "I'm getting older. Someday, I'll retire. But letting someone else run my schools? Not yet."

Dr. Pat is waiting for a response, but both Steve and the General stay quiet.

"When I retired," I say, "I shifted gears completely and left science behind. I became a yoga teacher, which wasn't an easy thing to do in my late fifties. Becoming an English teacher was a little easier for the old body, but it's been a mental challenge. You would think that going from being an expert to being a complete beginner would be horrible. But it was the opposite. It was liberating. A sort of reincarnation, a chance to start over."

"It's getting dark. Shall we have something sweet?" Dr. Pat suggests, nodding toward the dessert table. "Before the explosions start?"

Maybe that last bit was a step too far, especially given Thai Buddhist beliefs. But for me, it's more than a metaphor. Letting go of one life and reinventing myself has been a gift.

But I won't press the point. Not my place, and besides, there's mango with sticky rice on the buffet table.

In the dessert-time conversational lull, we hear a rumbling percolation coming from the Gulf. The first of the fireworks displays has begun, far enough away that conversation would be no problem, if we were still talking. But close enough, and colorful enough, and against a dark enough sky, that I can't help joining the chorus of oohs and aahs over the grand finale.

Because this is a competition, one grand finale is followed by the next overture of light and color. This is our entertainment for the evening, and further conversation isn't necessary.

This weekend in Pattaya is by far the most time we've spent with grown-up Thai people. Dr. Pat and the General are generous hosts. The more I get to know them, the more I respect them, their work, and their relationship. As the weekend progresses, we'll chat about our families, our tastes in music, and current events. But we won't revisit the topic of work, retirement, and making life meaningful as we age. These are the key topics for the four of us, but they are awkward ones. And, despite my growing affection, the awkwardness will remain.

A Big Cut

Bless me, Lord Buddha, for I am a mess. It's been ten weeks since my last haircut. And bless *you*, Lord Buddha, for the dearth of mirrors in Pathum Thani. A more self-reflective setting would be a hellish torment.

"Stephen," I say—Steve becomes Stephen when situations get serious—"we need haircuts. ASAP."

Neither Steve nor I have ever been mistaken for a fashion plate. Simple and easy have always been our style, both in clothing and in hair. But here our personal grooming routines are out of whack, and we need to get back on track.

"Pronoun," he replies, using Seidel shorthand for "speak for yourself, I'm fine." His hair is as much of a disaster as mine, but he'll deal with it when he's ready.

Me (first-person singular), I'm ready. But am I willing and able? For fifteen years, I had a standing appointment in Washington every fifth Wednesday with Ann. She knows exactly how to cut my hair—short, but not too short—and how to keep discreetly silent about the ever-increasing ratio of salt- to pepper-colored cuttings at her feet. Am I willing to trust anyone else?

Willing or un, this must be done. At this stage in my life, and here in Thailand where a head of snowy hair is as rare as an actual snowflake, letting my hair grow into a lank gray hank is not an option.

Am I able? This is the real question. Having made little progress in speaking Thai, I still rely heavily on body language to communicate. I know just enough numbers to understand prices, just enough food vocabulary to order a few dishes, and just enough polite phrases to compliment the cook. I doubt that going "snip snip" with my fingers will suffice to tell a Pathum Thani stylist how Ann does her magic. My best bet is a Bangkok salon where the staff is accustomed to dealing with language-challenged *farangs*.

In the city on a Saturday morning, after overindulging at the breakfast buffet, I leave Steve to digest in our hotel room. "Wish me luck," I say and head to BigCut in the huge shopping center adjoining the hotel. The salon's English name and row upon row of styling stations give me hope of being understood.

Indeed, the smiling host understands me perfectly, quotes the bargain price of three hundred baht for a haircut, and escorts me to the shampooing area. No need to talk here. I relax and let well-trained fingers massage my neck and scalp. With my eyes closed and the sound of the warm water running, I could be anywhere.

Walking to the styling area, I notice that, while all the stylists are women (though some may be ladyboys—Bangkok is famously open-minded regarding gender and sexuality), most of the customers are Thai men. *Mai pen rai.* I like their haircuts! Short on the sides, longer on top, all shaped with precision. Not exactly my standard style, but close enough.

My stylist's excellent posture, clean black smock, and neat row of scissors, clippers, and combs all telegraph competence.

"How would you like your hair?" she asks in lovely English.

I glance around the room and point to a young man with

a nice do. The microscopic furrowing of the stylist's eyebrows suffices to remind me of the Thai no-pointing rule. I lift my chin in the man's direction and tell her, "Just like that."

She takes my glasses off, and I close my eyes again as she sets to work. I feel my shoulders relax under the plastic cape and a wave of gratitude washes over me. I trust this stranger, a completely unexpected gift. Fifteen minutes later, she hands me back my glasses.

The woman in the mirror looks ten years younger than the one who walked into BigCut half an hour ago, and the smile on her face subtracts another five.

"Aroi mak mak kha!" I tell the stylist, whose perfectly penciled eyebrows rise and whose perfectly glossed lips turn up at the corners, as if attached to the brows. I add double thumbs up, and her own smile broadens to reveal her perfectly aligned teeth.

Back at the hotel, I apply a little lipstick of my own and can't stop looking in the bathroom mirror. Steve comes up behind me and says, "Great haircut! I guess they understood what you wanted. They spoke English?"

"They did. But I didn't. No need to. It was so easy."

For years, I wondered what I'd do when Ann retires and I need to find a new stylist. Now I know. If I can walk into a salon in Bangkok and trust a professional to do her job, I can do the same back home. But I won't be home for months, and I'll need a few more haircuts first.

Maybe I'll try a more authentically Thai experience at a Pathum Thani salon next time. Maybe Steve will come along. And maybe we'll manage to say something more appropriate than "it's very delicious" to express our appreciation.

Bending Over Backward
and Letting Go

"Here we are!" we announce in unison. The Thai woman who spotted me on the sidewalk, guessed where I was going, and guided me through this mazelike mini-mall laughs at our spontaneous duet. She obviously knows this place well. Does she wonder at my instant familiarity with this cubbyhole studio in Thonglor, a Bangkok neighborhood I've never visited? Can she imagine how these lavender walls and shelves of precisely folded blankets and neatly stacked blocks almost replicate the Maryland yoga studio where I've studied for the past twenty years?

Almost, but not quite. Crossing the threshold of that studio and leaving the concerns of the day outside meant instant bodily relaxation. That studio was my second home, and it's one of the first places I'll return to when our stint in Thailand is over. Now, as I cross this threshold, my heart rate quickens as the adrenaline surges. I need to take a deep breath simply to thank this woman, who introduces herself as Arada.

I need several more deep breaths when I approach the reception desk. There stands Howard, the studio director. He looks just like his photo on the studio's website, with his white hair and gentle eyes. He even seems to be wearing the same gray T-shirt. I chose this Sunday morning class expressly because Howard would be teaching, in English, but I didn't expect to see him working the front desk. I assumed I'd fill out a form, pay the class fee, set up my mat, and maybe exchange a smile or a few whispered words with another student before Howard made his entrance at the top of the hour.

That's how things work at home. It's what my mentor Martha does, because it's what our studio director does. When they see someone new in class, they say hello and ask for pertinent information—Iyengar yoga experience, injuries, illnesses.

Howard doesn't ask me any questions. I need to introduce myself. And I need to make a good impression. He doesn't know it, but this is a job interview. After class, I'm hoping to ask him about teaching opportunities here. I tell Howard about my yoga experience but don't mention my arthritic joints or that I haven't taken a class in more than two months.

I arrange my mat in the back corner of the room, though I know that Howard—like any good teacher—will be able to see me wherever I am. Howard begins class with a basic seated pose and chanting *om* three times, the standard opening of an Iyengar yoga class. We call it centering, and it really works. With your eyes closed, your posture upright, and the vibration of the chant filling the room, there's a shift.

My heart rate slows and my breath becomes smoother. This is what yoga is about. On a good day, that centered feeling lasts the whole class and sticks around for a while afterward.

Not today. With our first pose, my hope of impressing Howard flies out the window. He has us lie on our backs with a dense cork block the size of a kid's shoebox between our shoulder blades. This chest opener is a sure sign that he'll be teaching backbends.

For years backbends made me dizzy, sometimes even nauseated, until I learned how to use props—blocks, chairs, and blankets—to make them marginally approachable. But I don't have those things in Pathum Thani, and my body needs to get reacquainted with the block penetrating my back. I take a deep breath. Then another. My only goal now is to get through this class, one breath at a time.

"Inhale. Take your arms up, elbows straight, palms facing each other, fingertips toward the ceiling." Howard's instructions could be those of any Iyengar yoga teacher anywhere in the world, and I know they are meant to position our shoulders to maximize the effect of the block. "Exhale. Reach overhead, use your arms to lengthen both sides of the torso evenly," he says, clearly articulating each step in this stage of the pose. The longer Howard keeps us here, the more my caved chest opens and my hunched back unhunches, as the block transforms from an obstacle to a support.

Next Howard has us lie on our bellies for locust pose. He takes care to instruct us how to align our legs to avoid pinching in the lower back before he has us lift our legs and upper bodies off the floor, our arms alongside our torsos, into what some yoga teachers call Superman pose.

In this position, unlike the last, I can see the rest of the class—a half dozen slender, youthful Thai people and another half dozen less slender, less youthful *farangs*. There are a couple of beautiful locusts here, but I'm relieved that I'm not the only person whose pose is more dying cicada than Man of Steel. On the mat next to mine, Arada looks pained as she struggles to raise her legs.

"Arada," Howard says, "internally rotate your thighs, then move your tailbone toward your heels." Whether it's Howard's English or the subtle actions he's instructing that are difficult for Arada to understand, I feel for her.

Shock overtakes sympathy when Howard says, "Dian, stay where you are. Everyone else come watch." Nice that Howard remembers my name, but is he really going to use me, of all people, to demonstrate a backbend?

"Raise your left leg," he tells me. This isn't an easy action for me either, but with Howard's and a dozen other pairs of eyeballs fixed on my body, I will my left leg into the air. "Now, watch," he tells the other eyeballs, "as she moves her back inner upper left thigh to the outer thigh." My left thigh rotates obediently. As he continues his instructions, my legs, tailbone, and shoulders all move into alignment for locust pose.

This is what happens when teachers use me to demo. My sloppy, uncomfortable pose transforms into something that can teach other people, and teach me, what the pose is supposed to be. It's what happens when I teach a class, too. When I know that students are watching, I rise to the challenge.

Surely Howard could see that backbends aren't my strong suit. I've had to learn how to avoid pain and injury. I imagine Howard could see that, too, and I'd like to think that's why he picked me to demonstrate. My struggles as a yoga student are my strength as a yoga teacher. I can relate to others who struggle, and sometimes I can help them.

Howard sends the class back to their mats and repeats, practically verbatim, the instructions he just gave me.

"Much better, Arada," Howard says. "Much better, everyone." I'm going to take a tiny bit of credit for all these lovelier locusts.

An hour and a half ago, I entered this studio holding tight to a desire to teach. Then came the block and the backbends, and I let that desire go, not willingly but of necessity. But if it hadn't been the backbends, it would have been something else.

I'm far from my peak yoga form, and I should be practicing more—more often and more diligently—not teaching. When, with Howard's guidance, I focused on the task at hand rather than my desire to teach, back bending became more accessible, and an opportunity to teach arose.

For me, this is yoga. Little moments on the mat illuminate life lessons. The illumination doesn't last long, but if I keep coming back to the mat, there's a good chance the light will shine again.

"I hope you'll come back," Howard says as I leave the studio.

I do too.

Role-playing

All week long, to the tune of *Twinkle, Twinkle, Little Star*, the class has been singing:
Red and orange, green and blue
Shiny yellow, purple too
All the colors that we know
Live up in the rainbow

They sing it together at circle time, some sing solos at lunch, and I hear snatches of the melody from almost-napping K1s on their quilts.

"You all know the rainbow song well," I congratulate the children. "And I think you know *Rain, Rain, Go Away*, too." At this, they launch into the chorus, each shouting out their own name to let me know they want to play.

The first Friday in December is Arts Day at Pathum Thani Prep. Two Fridays ago was Sports Day, and two Fridays before that was our Halloween party. The preparations for each Friday extravaganza are exhausting, but fortunately Teachers Miranda and Candace are happy to take charge.

For Arts Day, Miranda and Candace will turn the playground into an exhibition space, with finger paintings of cherry trees and collages of triangles on display for proud parents to admire. The kids will perform Thai and Chinese songs and dances under the batons of Khru Nok and Laoshi Ling. Teacher Steve is master of ceremonies and might even get a haircut for the occasion. In a moment of arts-inspired enthusiasm, I volunteered for the school play.

I am not a drama teacher. I have never written, produced, directed, or even had a bit part in a play. But I was a meteorologist. We've been studying weather words in class, though it's been a challenge to teach about rain and snow here in central Thailand's dry season. Since we arrived in Pathum Thani, there has been no measurable precipitation of any kind, and the rainy season is months away. Actual atmospheric conditions notwithstanding, and with faith in the magic of theater, I've scripted a one-act play titled "A Rainy Day," with three short scenes and roles for all the children.

"Are you ready to put your lines together with the songs in our play? Who has practiced at home?" I ask hopefully. All hands shoot up.

Scene 1—We Need Rain

"I need Pepper, Golf, and Ivy onstage," I announce. These children have the most challenging speaking parts—four lines each. If they can manage Scene 1, we'll be in good shape for the rest of the play.

The kids hop up the wooden steps to the platform on the playground. I point out their marks on the stage, bits of masking tape with their names in block lettering. With a grand sweep of my arms, I show where our audience will be and, in what I imagine is a theatrical voice, say, "On stage, we are actors. As actors, we must look at our audience and use our best outdoor voices." Pepper, Golf, and Ivy all nod in earnest agreement.

I don't doubt the importance of being earnest, but with four-year-olds it is no guarantee of success, and this first rehearsal is a disaster. Nobody's voice goes above a whisper, and all three actors need reminders of their lines—even Golf, the class brainiac. Slowly, with continual prompts, they manage to speak the dialogue that reveals the dramatic tension that I so carefully constructed—the farmer's crops need water, the child yearns to play in puddles, the city dweller pleads for cleaner, cooler air. But then Chompoo, a theatrical prodigy at age two, floats, perfectly cloudlike, onto the stage, and the threesome nails the Greek chorus: "Little Cloud, we need rain! Please may we have some rain?"

Scene 2—The Rainy Day

The dramatic arc reaches its climax in the second scene, when several more students join the action.

"Thunder and Lightning, onstage, please," I call. Chet and Nin mount the steps and, though their routes are roundabout, eventually find their marks. "Mung Bean and Corn, come on up," and, nudged by their classmates, up come Sai and Panit. This climatic (bad pun intended) scene features a riotous rainstorm followed by joyful thanks. Hoping that enthusiasm for toy drums and flashlights will carry the day, I've given these children nonspeaking roles and let the Narrator (a.k.a. director, playwright, stage manager, yours truly) relate the story.

Small in stature but big on drama, Chompoo is especially convincing as a mushrooming cumulonimbus, waving her arms and jumping higher and higher, while Chet gleefully beats his drum as the thunder god. Nin creates lightning with his two-fisted flashlights, although the midday sun utterly overwhelms our attempt at theatrical lighting.

Panit (as a corn kernel) and Sai (mung bean seed) are supposed to begin at ground level, in dormant states. Sai, who frequently seems to inhabit her own fantasy world, is happy to nestle into a ball on the stage, but Panit's muscular body is built for action, and he jumps off the stage and dashes to the playground. With Candace's help, we plant Panit back onstage in our make-believe cornfield next to Sai's mung bean patch. Our raincloud, Chompoo, skips across the stage and pretends to sprinkle the crops with water, and, with a bit of nudging, cornstalks and mung beans are reaching skyward in admirable growth spurts.

Scene 3—A Rainbow

"Athit, Lek, and Pichai, take your places, please," I call. Now the entire kindergarten is onstage, more or less on their appointed marks. I raise my arm to give the four-count and the class sings a roaring rendition of *Rain, Rain Go Away*.

Athit beams as the Sun, and this sight alone is worth all my effort, while Lek and Pichai fumble with their rolled paper banner. Candace has gone to great lengths to mix all the required colors from the red, blue, and yellow poster paints in the classroom art cabinet, and this rainbow prop is far and away our most sophisticated bit of scenery.

I narrate: "Everyone was amazed to see a beautiful rainbow! With their backs to the sun, they watched the rain and marveled at all the colors." With so many bodies crowding the stage, the boys struggle to unfurl the rainbow, which twists and droops decidedly undramatically to the ground. But that doesn't dampen our spirits as we all sing *Red and orange, green and blue...*

Epilogue

Two more rehearsals, then Arts Day, which goes by in a blur. Lying in bed Friday night, I replay the day and our play. The missed cues and misplaced props. The laughter. Panit falling off the stage. The gasps. The adoring standing-room-only audience with its multitude of cameras recording every utterance. Best of all, the standing ovation from the crowd of parents, grandparents, siblings, nannies, and Dr. Pat.

I hear a tapping outside. It grows louder and more insistent. Could it be? Opening the door, I feel the wind in my face and raindrops on my outstretched hand. I step outside to watch lightning flash against the clouds. Rain wets my head and shoulders in this, my first, and my last, rainstorm in Pathum Thani. On the night of my first, and last, play.

There will be no rainbow this night. For that, we would need the sun, and Athit, I hope, is snug in bed. But I have no doubt that tomorrow we'll have puddles, cleaner air, and, if we're lucky, some relief from the heat.

On Saturday morning, I can't detect any change in the air quality, and there are no puddles on the *soi*. Steve doesn't even remember the storm, and if it weren't for the damp towels on our clothesline, he could persuade me that I dreamt it. But I'm convinced that, though we didn't conjure a Little Cloud in Pathum Thani's dry season, we got rain, and that, like the farmer's corn and mung beans, we all have grown a bit taller.

The General Is Always on Duty

The General approaches slowly, clearly in pain and relying heavily on his cane.

"It's not serious," he tells us, waving off our worries. "The doctor recommends surgery. But not now. Now, I have work to do. Perhaps you can help?"

The General has never asked us for anything. He has always been the generous host—showing us the lay of the land as de facto chair of our welcoming committee, treating us to a weekend in Pattaya, asking after our welfare whenever we cross paths on campus. If we ever needed anything, he told us the day we arrived in Pathum Thani, we had only to call. "I am always on duty," he said with a smile.

It wasn't until several weeks later that we learned his surname, Sarasin. Thai given names and surnames can be supercalifragilisticexpialidociously long and are reserved for official matters like birth certificates. Instead, everyone goes by a single nickname. We still don't know our students' surnames or those of any of the Thai teachers at school. They will forever be Lek, Golf, Som, and Nok to us.

Though relatively short as surnames go, Sarasin seems to be a big one in these parts. Pathum Thani Prep is on Soi Sarasin. The huge tract of land that the family owns is Thailand in miniature, with all the essential elements—not just our school and apartment building, but businesses, houses, rice fields, a pretty little *wat*, and a military training camp as well. What possible help could he need from us?

The ministry—he doesn't say which ministry, but I assume he means defense—has asked him to serve on a national commission. Their remit: climate change and water resources.

That first day in Pathum Thani, at lunch, the General seemed to have studied our résumés. He knew about Steve's environmental policy experience and about my research in climate science. I assumed he was being a polite host and that the nature of our work wouldn't much interest a retired military man.

"I am not an expert," he tells us. "You are experts. Can you help me find people who have studied what climate change could mean for my country? People to advise the commission?"

Like many tropical places, Thailand is especially vulnerable to climate variations.

"This year," the General tells us, "Thailand is facing her worst drought in forty years. The monsoon rains arrived late and left early. Rice and sugar farmers have lost their crops, and hydropower generation is at risk. We are worried about the future and need to prepare."

He's right to be worried. Thailand is already hot and humid, and Bangkok ranks high on every list of the world's sultriest cities. Much of the country, including its coastlines, islands, and capital—low-lying Bangkok, the Venice of the East—will be inundated as sea levels rise.

Though the subject is grim, I'm thrilled by the opportunity to reciprocate the General's many kindnesses. Steve and I may be beyond our depth teaching kindergarten, but researching climate change and networking with climate experts is familiar territory.

It's also one of the few ways we can truly be useful in Thailand.

Though Dr. Pat seems happy with our work at Prep, and so do the children's parents, I'm not convinced we are making much of a difference. We imagined teaching English to public school kids with limited prospects. Instead, we're teaching children from professional families that can afford the tuition (on par with US private schools) at a kindergarten with ample resources and a four-to-fourteen teacher-student ratio. (When we arrived at Prep in October, there were three kids in K1 and eight in K2. Now in December enrollment is up by three.)

What motivates us to do the work we do? In my case, and Steve's too, youthful idealism made us choose environmental work. Science suited my analytic mind, and Steve, the practical problem solver, gravitated toward the policy world, but we both felt duty-bound to apply our skills to real-world problems.

I know little about the General's career—much less than he knows about mine—or how he chose, *if* he chose, his military life. But I believe him when he says that he is always on duty. Even in retirement, he is not letting an ailing body keep him from serving his country.

Duty no longer motivates Steve and me. We both trust that others are working on the problems that dominated our lives for decades. Or perhaps it's more accurate to say that our sense of duty has shifted. Now we feel an obligation to explore and engage with the wider world, and to do so today. Because we know that the cane, the pain, or the surgeon might be knocking on our door tomorrow.

Start, and Stop,
Spreading the News

"What did you two have for breakfast? Giggle pills?" asks Candace just before lunchtime on a hot December day. I look at Steve, he looks at me, and we both see what she sees in our faces: irrepressible joy.

"We just got some nice news from home," I say.

"Let me guess," Candace says. "Rose is engaged."

"Huh?" Steve says. "How did you know?"

Our first week at school, we showed the class a few photos of the family, including our daughter Rose. The kids weren't much interested in the people, but they were charmed by a video clip of our cat Minerva jumping up to a sunny windowsill and settling down to bask. It's hardly a contender for a World's Cutest Kitty Video contest, but they insisted on watching it over and over, as if they'd never seen a house cat before. When Steve asked if anyone had pets, almost all the children had a story. Except for Sai's unicorn, whose name she claimed is Meow, I'm still unsure which of their animals were living creatures, plush toys, or imaginary friends.

Since then, we haven't spoken about Rose to our coteachers. Though they are about the same age, late twenties, their lives are so different, and comparisons could be uncomfortable. So I'm surprised that Candace even remembers Rose's name.

But today I throw privacy out the window. "She just called from New York. It's almost midnight there. Her boyfriend proposed. Right outside Lincoln Center, on bended knee. Look, here's a photo." The moment, like most every moment these days, was recorded for posterity. The cellphone photo, taken by a random passerby, is poorly lit and out of focus, but the smiles on their faces shine brightly.

"Oh, they seem so happy! Congratulations!" exclaims Candace. "What sort of wedding are they planning?"

"No idea," says Steve. "But they promised they'd wait until we're back from Thailand. That's all that matters."

"I know exactly where I want to get married."

I take her bait. "Do tell."

"On a wine estate in Stellenbosch," says Candace, who left South Africa three years ago to teach in Thailand. "With Blushing Bride protea flowers for the bouquet."

"Sounds perfectly lovely," I say, wondering if Candace has a fiancé to go with the venue, floral arrangements, and wine selections.

Candace spends most weekends with friends in Bangkok. Over the past few months, during tidy-up time—the half hour after the children leave school—she's told Miranda and us about the jazz clubs and discos she visits and some of the people, from all over the world, she's met. But she hasn't mentioned any steady romantic interest.

A generous, gregarious personality, Candace has invited Steve and me to join her on weekends when our trips to Bangkok have intersected with hers. Mostly, we've declined, because her nights on the town begin hours after we're in bed. But a few weeks ago, we met her on a Sunday afternoon for an early supper (brunch for Candace) at a vegetarian restaurant she thought I'd like on Sukhumvit Road. She was right. It's now on my short-list of favorite Bangkok eateries. The rough wood furniture and philodendrons in macramé plant hangers remind me of my Berkeley days, as does the best secondhand bookshop in the city just across the street. I'll try to replicate the restaurant's vegan broccoli quinoa burger when I'm back in a kitchen with a stove. Some of the waiters knew Candace, but she met us alone.

"Have you met someone special recently?" I ask.

"I'm working on that part," laughs Candace, with a wink.

A few hours later, during tidy-up time, Miranda approaches the classroom sink, where I'm washing poster paints from four-teen orange nylon bibs, the all-purpose protective garments we use for everything from painting to cooking to gardening.

"Candace told me your great news. Congratulations!" she says with a half smile. "Were you surprised?"

"Yes and no," I say. "Elliot gave us a heads-up. Actually called a few days ago and asked for our blessing. So gracious, and so sweet. But we didn't know when he planned to propose. When the phone rang today and we saw the call was from Rose—she rarely calls, and we rarely call her—well, we had a pretty good idea why she was calling."

"Really? No phone calls?" Miranda asks. "Let me show you my phone plan. Very cheap. I can call my family in the Philippines whenever I want."

I have no intention of changing plans. Our phone plans are already the most complicated detail of our life in Thailand, and the less I have to deal with Thai TrueMove the better. But I let Miranda show me the app because I don't want to tell her that what limits our phone calls isn't the cost but how seldom our daughter wants to chat.

"I don't know what I'd do without this phone," Miranda

says. "I've been here for eight years, and I've been home only twice. Flights are so expensive. But at least I can call. What's the English word? Lifeline? Or is that what connects a mother and baby? I mean a connection to everyone back home."

"Lifeline is good," I say. I pass on teaching Miranda *umbilical cord*, though she has asked me more than once for help with her English. Talking about belly buttons would break the mood. I had assumed Miranda was happy to be settled in Thailand. She's mentioned missing *lechon*, roasted suckling pig, but I had chalked that up to the generic, and ultimately inconsequential, culinary yearnings we all experience when far from home.

"I didn't know," I say.

"My boyfriend came to visit once, but it's expensive for him, too. We talk by phone whenever we can, but when he's at sea, even phone calls are impossible."

A boyfriend, at sea—this too is news to me. I don't want to pry, but I sense that she wants to talk. "What's his name?"

"Marius." And she does want to talk. She tells me Marius is a merchant marine, part of the huge world of Filipino overseas workers supporting families back home, including Miranda. While she has been in Pathum Thani, he has traveled the wide world, spending months at a time onboard cargo ships transporting goods from Asia to the West and returning with containers full of waste. They have been together for ten years. Together, but apart. Tears well up in her eyes.

And in mine. Miranda and Marius should not have to leave home to find decent jobs. *Their* parents should be looking forward to a wedding, maybe grandchildren. "I'm sorry, Miranda. For both of you."

In the evening, Steve and I talk. We're thankful our only

child is making a life for herself, that her fiancé, a new word in our vocabulary, is a real mensch whose company we enjoy, that he and Rose are happy together.

And we agree. No more giggle pills at school. No more talk of the engagement with our young colleagues, unless they ask. No need to flaunt.

But if they ask, we'll talk. We'll open up. We'll stop assuming they are like our daughter, fiercely guarding their privacy and keeping secrets.

Or rather, I will stop. Maybe if I stop expecting them to keep their personal lives personal, they'll feel more comfortable sharing them with me.

Or perhaps they won't. Candace and Miranda have been working together for a few years and are close. They confide in each other. Would they ever confide in me?

Am I a good listener? I try. My mother is definitely a good listener. "Maybe too good," she says, meaning that sometimes she tires of listening to people pour out their souls. I'm not too good. It's rare for people to pour out their souls to me. But if Candace or Miranda ever feels so inclined, I'll be here. Same goes for Rose.

Foster Care

The image could sport the tagline, "For just sixty-three cents per day, you can help save animals in crisis." Tracy's email message is disturbing enough, but her photo takes my breath away. Two hands grip Minnie's tiny body, and an elbow around her neck immobilizes her head. Her pupils are huge black holes perfectly centered in the wide-open yellow-gray eyes that look pleadingly directly into the camera. "If Steve sees this," I think, "we'll be on the next flight home."

But upon closer inspection, what seems to be terrorizing Minerva isn't a postsurgery cranial helmet but simply your standard, hand-crocheted, cat-sized turkey costume, complete with multicolored cockscomb, googly eyes, and a bright orange beak. We've never decked out our cat for Thanksgiving dinner, or any other holiday celebration, but at least the picture isn't evidence of animal abuse.

A generous reader could give Tracy's newsy message an even more positive spin. Tracy's daughter Zeenie and Minerva have bonded like superglue; Minerva is eating regularly (and vomiting just as regularly); and though she disappeared for more than a few anxious hours last month, Tracy's son eventually found her sleeping in his laundry hamper.

And then there's the bit about taking our indoor-only Minnie out with the family dog for walks around the neighborhood.

Again, not something we ever contemplated, but heck, we are nine thousand miles away, living a new lifestyle. Why shouldn't Minnie have a little adventure, too? At least they've got her on a leash. A leash?

"Steve?" I say, with some trepidation. "There's a message. From Tracy."

You might have thought I said that Rose was calling again or that Anthony Rendon would be sticking with our Nationals for another season after all. Steve needs to know the news. Now.

The moment his eyes meet Minnie's, Steve's open almost as wide as hers. His jaw drops, his brow furrows, and he exhales slowly as he reads the email. And then . . . uncontrollable laughter. I'm baffled, but Steve is doubled over.

And he can't stop. He can't inhale or exhale. I fear my husband might whoop his way to a heart attack.

I run to the kitchen sink for water, but when I bring it back, Steve's laughter only intensifies, which I wouldn't have thought possible. Struggling for breath, he raises his forearms and crosses them in front of his face. He nearly has to push me away to remind me that Thai tap water is a complete no-no.

By the time I return with bottled water, Steve has regained a measure of composure. But it is short-lived, and he ejects his first sip onto my computer, dowsing both Minerva and the keyboard.

"I'm sorry," Steve says when he finally collects himself. "I just kept picturing Minerva's new life. Nestling in a pile of dirty gym cloths, strutting around outside with Tracy's dog and her hens, dressed up in a turkey suit and purring in Zeenie's lap at Thanksgiving dinner. Then vomiting up mashed potatoes. I just lost it."

And he loses it again. I'm delighted that he sees the humor in all of this. My biggest concern while we've been away has been my mother's welfare, but Steve's has been Minerva's care and feeding. It's a relief that he's happy—maybe too happy—with her foster care.

I wipe the laptop, and there is Minerva, still staring at us.

Steve stares, too. His lips press together, his chin crinkles, his eyes blink, and a tear rolls down his cheek.

He tells me softly, "I just miss that warm little purring machine."

Wait till he sees what they do for Christmas.

Q&A at Tea

When the General phoned, Steve couldn't say no.

"The General's been so sweet," Steve says, "and now I think he wants to thank us for helping with his climate commission. He's inviting us to tea on Wednesday."

"With Dr. Pat?" I ask.

"Nope. He wants us to meet one of his old army buddies."

"Are you sure he wants *us*? This sounds like a guy thing."

"Pretty sure," Steve says. "Anyway, you need to come. The friend is also retired, and now he's a monk. The General said, 'You can ask him anything.'"

"About what?"

"I don't know. Life, the universe, how he likes his orange robes, anything."

"Forty-two," I snort.

We came to Thailand to teach English, not seeking spiritual enlightenment. But here we are, in an overwhelmingly Buddhist country, with an offer to meet someone who is devoting his life to his faith. Steve, who, if he had the choice, would limit his engagement with religion to weddings, bar and bat mitzvahs, and funerals, will have exactly zero questions for a Buddhist monk. But I'm a tad intrigued.

Through yoga, I've been exposed to the basics of Buddhism, though detangling the influences of Buddhism and Hinduism on yogic philosophy (or is it vice versa?) is well beyond me. So is the distinction between Theravada, the Thai branch of Buddhism, and other sects. Maybe this tea party will be our own private survey course: Thai Buddhism 101.

Although we've seen hundreds of monks—in the streets, on the subway, and in temples—we've never had a conversation with one, let alone taken tea together. There are strict rules for encounters with monks: keep your head below theirs; *wai* deeply when greeting them; don't point your feet at them; don't touch them. That last rule applies particularly to women. Monastic life in Thailand seems to be a male affair. We've yet to encounter a nun. The same goes for the military and the police; I can't recall seeing a single woman in uniform.

On Tuesday night, I can't sleep. I think of Ari, my serene, thoughtful ESOL student in Washington. I found his very monkhood unnerving, and that was on my own turf. This monk will be older, ex-military, maybe more intimidating. Or maybe more traditional, less comfortable talking with a woman. Will he want us to meditate? We might be able to manage that. Will he ask us to chant? Lord, I hope not—neither of us can carry a tune.

I need an agenda. In the dark, with Steve sleeping peacefully at my side, I mull over what I know, and what I don't know, about Buddhism. The problem is that I don't know what I don't know—those pesky unknown unknowns—but by dawn I've jotted three topics on a pad.

Meditation. How do Thai monks manage to sit comfortably on the floor in positions most *farangs* would find excruciating? Do they practice yoga? Or is it, as I suspect from observing our students, a natural result of starting young?

Social justice. Steve and I both view community activism as one of the better aspects of Western religions. Does the Buddhist focus on compassion translate to organized political engagement?

Reincarnation (and this is as far into woo-woo-land as I'm willing to go). Is the idea of being reborn in another form a comfort or a worry? Doesn't it take your focus off the here and now, and how does that jibe with mindfulness and living in the present moment?

At breakfast, as Steve slices our daily mango, I rewrite my notes more legibly. I'll keep them in my pocket all day.

That evening, the General greets us at the door of his home, which reminds me of a Mediterranean villa. We use the *wai* for equals—palms together, heads dipping to touch our lips to our fingertips—even though his military rank puts him near the apex of Thai society. Like us, he is in his sixties, and age matters in *wai* etiquette.

The monk is sitting on a straight-back wooden chair in the parlor, his round head shorn, his orange robes elegantly draping his upright frame. His glasses are like Ari's and give him an owl-ish expression. When we enter the room, the monk stands, and we offer him our most respectful *wai*, bowing more deeply this time, our thumbs touching our foreheads to acknowledge his wisdom.

The General gestures toward the upholstered settee (thought-fully putting us lower to the floor than the monk) and asks his housekeeper to bring tea.

"How are you liking Thailand?" the monk asks. His smile and this mundane question immediately put Steve and me at ease.

"We love Thailand," Steve answers. "We love how easily peo-ple smile, especially the children. I thought it was a trope for tourists, but Thailand really is the Land of Smiles, and it's conta-gious." The monk smiles more broadly and so does Steve.

"And we love the way people treat each other with respect," I chime in, layering on the goodwill. "And how *we* are treated with respect. Even our kindergarten students are respectful and kind." I chuckle. "Well, most of the time."

"Of course," replies the monk, without irony. "You are teachers."

And with that, the superficiality ends and our lesson begins. The monk doesn't ask us to meditate or to chant. He talks.

He begins with an accounting of his childhood, university studies in Germany and Switzerland, military career, and friendship with the General. Like many young Thai men, he ordained and spent a few months as a monk decades ago to make merit (and so accrue divine protection) for his mother. After retiring from the army, he reordained of his own volition.

"Why?" It's not one of my three questions, but the monk's pause seems to invite one of us to ask, and Steve is mum.

"I have much to learn," he says. What follows makes clear that he feels he has much to teach as well.

The monk lays out a warp of earthly concerns—pollution, poverty, disease—and we nod in agreement. His tapestry quickly becomes complex as he weaves in a weft of abstractions—impermanence, the eightfold path, detachment, awakening. Like a mechanical mannequin, I smile and nod at regular intervals. Following the threads requires a keener mind, or maybe just a better foundation in Buddhism, than I possess.

Steve is, uncharacteristically, savoring his tea, and his relaxed posture signals he's content to let the monk carry the conversational burden. The General, who said the monk would entertain questions, is also silent. Though I'd like to take the conversation back to firmer ground, I'm concerned that the issues I lost sleep over are too pedestrian to raise now.

Around the parlor, framed family photos are on every table-top. Here is the General with Dr. Pat and their children. There he is in uniform, in his younger days. An even older photo shows another man, but with the General's stance and broad face, looking sharp and serious in his own highly decorated dress uniform.

The three pillars of what's called "Thai-ness" are the nation, religion, and the monarchy. But even a casual student of Thai government and society knows that the military is in charge here. Thailand has seen more military coups than any other country in modern history, a dozen in the past century, and the current government is headed by a retired general who first came to power in one of those coups.

This family has been in the top ranks for decades, and I'm guessing the General was raised in privilege. Maybe the monk was too. Surely not every young man in Thailand has the opportunity to study in Europe. It's hard for me to reconcile wealth with a military career. And it's hard to reconcile the monk's life in the army with his current monastic life. Or are both simply different sides of the same coin—different forms of devotion, regimentation, or commitment to service?

The tea grows cold, and the light in the parlor grows pinkish and dims. The monk says he must be up early tomorrow morning, and every morning, and he thanks us for an enjoyable evening. We thank him for speaking with us. We thank the General for his hospitality. He thanks us for coming. We ask him to give our regards to Dr. Pat. This is as much conversation as we've had all evening.

The following day, I'm awake well before dawn trying to make sense of the tea party, and I decide to attempt a seated meditation before my yoga practice. I imagine the monk is up early, too, meditating or chanting. I imagine the General taking tea, maybe with his wife, maybe in their parlor. I try to put those images aside and focus on my breath, but tidbits of the monk's lecture keep interfering. I'm not comfortable. I fidget. Thai Buddhism 101 has left me more unsettled than serene.

Crossing Borders

"Lord willing, we'll be renewed," says the young mother outside the gate of the Thai consulate in Vientiane, Laos. "Thailand is where we are meant to be."

The enormity of the sunhat shading her freckled face suggests her dermatologist might disagree, but the look she exchanges with her husband and the squeeze she gives their young son's hand tell me she is speaking their truth. Steve and I, in our own high-SPF headgear, might put it differently, and others in the crowd are putting it differently in a half dozen languages. But we all share this American Alice's visa anxiety.

Khru Nok spent weeks preparing our paperwork. Our signatures are the only words we can read on the dozen or so neatly completed forms, all stamped and signed by bureaucrats from multiple Thai ministries. We hold tight to our fat manila envelopes, our appointment numbers (211 and 215), our authenticated college diplomas in their DIY cardboard portfolio, and our hopes of extending our tenure at Pathum Thani Prep for another ninety days.

"And what do you folks do in Thailand?" Steve asks the woman.

He hardly needed to ask, and I imagine he did so mainly to hear more of Alice's pleasant voice and Minnesota Nice English. They are missionaries in Udon Thani. They set out before dawn for the one-hour road trip and crossed the Mekong River at the Thai-Lao Friendship Bridge in time to see the sunrise.

Our one-hour flight from Bangkok crossed the Mekong at thirty thousand feet. The idea of two ten-hour overnight bus rides for a visa run was more than we could stomach.

As the sun climbs over the Lao capital, the crowd outside the consulate swells to hundreds. Beads of sweat balloon on every brow, though early morning in Vientiane seems a teaspoon cooler than early morning in Pathum Thani. There, our class will have already raised the Thai flag and sung the anthem and might just now be sitting for morning meditation.

At nine o'clock sharp, a uniformed officer, clipboard in hand, announces, "Applicants with numbers 1 through 50 may enter. Please have your documents ready."

A Thai consular official in the Lao People's Democratic Republic addresses a multinational group, and what language does she speak? This umpteenth proof that English is a—no, *the*—global language is reassurance that teaching English for Speakers of Other Languages is a worthwhile vocation for our retirement years. It's hardly missionary work, but I'd like to think it checks the doing-good-in-the-world box.

"Forty-two," says Alice, pulling out her appointment card. "We're up."

"That's auspicious," Steve says, though I doubt she'll get the reference. She doesn't strike me as the sci-fi type. "Good luck."

"God bless you," she replies, making momentary eye contact with each of us.

The officer unlocks the metal gate and checks each person's appointment number as she allows the first fifty to file through.

In the rearranged crowd, I recognize a slender man holding number 261.

"Weren't you on our flight from Bangkok yesterday?"

"Yes, ma'am," he says. "I've seen a few others here, too."

Mr. 261 is an engineer at a solar panel company in Bangkok.
"There sure is plenty of sunshine in Thailand. Here too," I
say, squinting in the glare. "Is solar energy a growth industry in
this part of the world?"

"I hope so. For my career, but more importantly for the
Earth. My name is Martin," he says as he pulls a pamphlet from
his backpack. "Do you know about Extinction Rebellion?"

Martin was born and raised in Jakarta, went to university in
Melbourne, and is determined to save the planet.

"We have to act now," he says. "We're in a climate crisis,
which could mean the extinction of the human race!"

"You're right," I say, which is all Martin needs to hear.

None of his pitch is news to me, but I don't interrupt. He
hits all the key points: heat waves, droughts, wildfires, sea-level
rise, health impacts, economic displacement, environmental ref-
ugees. Alice may have spared us her evangelism, but Martin is on
a mission.

He doesn't need to convert us. Steve and I both devoted our
careers to the climate issue. We thought we were checking the
doing-good-in-the-world box then, too. But the problem we
tried to address remains unsolved. Not just unsolved but much
harder to solve, because humans have pushed the climate into
uncharted territory, and there is no pathway for pushing it back.

"But why leave Indonesia for Thailand?" I ask. "Aren't the
climate risks similar?"

"Yes," he says. "Both are tropical countries, already hot, with
lots of people in vulnerable coastal areas. But the *social* climates
are completely different. Indonesia will be a political tinderbox
when climate conditions become difficult. People will take to

the streets. Thailand is hot, but Thai people are cool. You know, *mai pen rai.*"

Again I agree. Since arriving in Thailand, I have yet to witness a Thai person over age five get anxious or upset. Not even bureaucrats. The consular staff this morning is casual and courteous as they control the sidewalk crowd. If there's one Thai trait I'd like to adopt, it's the *mai pen rai* take on life.

Just after ten thirty, the consular officer calls numbers 201 to 250.

"Good luck," Martin says.

"Good luck to you," I say, "with your visa and your work." I don't say "God bless you," though that's what I'm thinking.

Inside the consulate courtyard, Steve and I are relieved to find a canopy shading rows of applicants, seated in numerical order, waiting to be called to the window.

And by eleven thirty, our paperwork, our passports, and our fate for the next ninety days are out of our hands.

We spend the afternoon exploring the languid Lao capital, where communist hammer-and-sickle flags fly alongside the national flag. Vientiane has none of Bangkok's noise, crowds, or traffic. There's a soft, warm breeze at the night market as we watch the sunset over the Thai side of the Mekong. There is no boat traffic on the river, and the water is dark and peaceful. But I won't be able to relax until we learn our visa status.

As instructed, we return at one thirty the next afternoon, judgment time. We see a few familiar faces in the courtyard, but not Alice's or Martin's.

Soon our numbers are called. Our paperwork has passed muster, and our passports have new visas for another three months in Thailand.

On our way out, the officer advises us, "Your visas are valid for one entry. If you're planning any other trips outside the king-dom, be sure to get reentry permits before your departure from Thailand."

That evening, at the gate for our Bangkok-bound flight, I spot Martin, looking miserable.

"Problems with your visa?" I ask.

"No, I got it," he replies. "Just feeling guilty about these flights. A one-hundred-kilogram carbon footprint for a piece of paper. I should have taken the bus."

And now I feel guilty, too, and not just about tonight's flight or the taxi we'll take from the airport back to Pathum Thani. In my life, I've probably been responsible for more CO_2 emissions than several entire Thai or Lao villages.

Alice's little boy and our kindergarten students will have to face the consequences. Their prayers might be comforting, and a *mai pen rai* attitude might keep anxiety at bay. But, as Martin knows, we are crossing the frontier to a grim future. And there will be no reentry permits.

Doing the Pinocchio

The star, smack dab in the center of the classroom's January calendar, is smudgy with little fingerprints. Tomorrow is Pathum Thani Prep's much-anticipated outing to one of the province's top attractions, the National Geological Museum, and Head Teacher Miranda has assembled the teaching team to review field trip rules.

1. Students must wear school uniforms and lanyards with name tags.
2. Everyone must travel to and from the museum with the class, in the school bus.
3. Everyone must stay in assigned groups.
4. Parents may not accompany the class.
5. Everyone must bring a lunch and water bottle.

"Fourteen students, four teachers. Here are the groupings," continues Miranda. She generously assigns herself and Candace four students each, including Panit and Pepper, the two most likely to scamper away. In lieu of a fourth student, Steve and I will tote gear. "Teacher Steve will take the lunches to the cafeteria when we arrive. Teacher Dian will carry the first-aid kit, including the emergency contact list. Keep it with you at all times." I nod my agreement and hope to heaven my tourniquet-tying skills won't be tested.

The next morning, fourteen parents (mostly mothers) and a

few grandparents chat and snap photos from outside the school gate as we assemble the children. A white van is parked in the school driveway. The van has seating, and seatbelts, for eleven. Including our driver, my quick headcount puts us at nineteen.

Miranda exchanges a few words with the driver.

"I'll be back soon," she tells us before hurrying to the *rong rian*, where I assume she'll ask Dr. Pat for a bigger bus. Candace turns to the children and says, "How about a song for your parents?"

"*You Are My Sunshine?*" suggests Chet. This latest addition to our repertoire has quickly risen to the top of the Prep hit parade. After several repetitions of the two verses we've learned, Miranda hasn't returned.

Candace, who always knows how to engage the kids and please their parents, has a brilliant idea—*Let's Do the Pinocchio*. We know plenty of choruses, enough that several moms eventually join in on the chorus of "Everybody in, everybody out, everybody turn around, everybody shout, Hey!" By the time Miranda returns, there's a dance party happening at the gate.

With determined composure, Miranda assigns each teacher a seat in the white van and then assigns each teacher's lap a student. I am in the center of the third row, with Sai on my lap, Chet and Ivy to my right, two other children to my left, and the first-aid kit between my feet. Steve is in the second row with a similar arrangement of little bodies.

If, years ago, I had ever seen my daughter and her classmates sardine-packed into a van like this, I would have pulled her off, complained to the driver, and raised a stink first with the teacher, then with the principal. Steve would have done the same, I think. Or at least I hope. I tap his shoulder and whisper, "Seriously?"

"AOPG," he says, shaking his head.

I could have anticipated his response, Above Our Pay Grade,

but that doesn't make biting my tongue any less painful. Have these Thai parents signed on to AOPG, too? Not one is complaining. Not one is raising a stink. I know that conflict avoidance is practically part of the Thai genetic code, but I would have thought maternal instincts would trump social norms.

Their children seem equally unperturbed. They've surely seen entire families loaded onto scooters on local roads, even if their own families travel by car. The kids are gleeful and eager to get going. Except for Chet. Outside the window his mother is smiling and waving goodbye, but a shadow is settling on his face.

Chet turns to me to say, "Teacher Dian, you and Sai need to fasten your seatbelt and prepare for takeoff." Would that I could, my little friend. Would that I could.

Our driver's familiarity with local roads seems minimal, and our expected thirty-minute ride takes almost an hour. We sing *You Are My Sunshine* at least three more times—and each repetition temporarily brings a smile back to Chet's anxious face—before we exhaust our repertoire.

We eventually arrive safely and more than ready to stretch our legs. We find just a handful of other visitors at the museum, so we have the huge, well-curated galleries to ourselves. The highlight is the dinosaur display with life-size, vocalizing, robotic replicas of extinct reptiles. A few of the boys recognize and can name several species that are featured in our classroom's dinosaur book. But no one, not even Golf, knows about Thailand's own Siamotyrannus and Siamosaurus.

"Did they live in Pathum Thani, Teacher Steve?" he asks. Golf looks to Steve not just because he is part of Steve's field trip trio. Golf has come to consider Steve a polymath expert on every aspect of the natural world, probably because Steve likes to include odd bits of trivia in his K2 lessons.

Biggest species of mammal? Some kids guessed water buffaloes and tigers, but Golf knew. Blue whale.

World's tallest mountain? Lek, whose family recently visited Japan, remembered Mount Fuji, but Golf said, "No, Mount Everest." "Good guess," said Teacher Steve, "but Mauna Kea is taller if you measure from the center of the Earth." Golf would have a gem for his dad that evening when he asked about Golf's day at school.

Asia's hottest city? I discouraged this discussion, for lack of a peer-reviewed reference and because it might well be Bangkok, which is too depressing to consider.

But Steve doesn't know the first thing about Thai dinosaurs, and the museum guide is unwilling to speculate.

"Sorry, Golf, we just don't know," Steve says, leaving Golf speechless and with a newly empty pedestal.

By the time we have eaten lunch, used the toilets, and packed up, I still have my threesome—Chet, Ivy, and Sai—and our first-aid kit is blessedly unopened. Miranda approaches to whisper that, while we were wandering through the Early Cretaceous, Chet's mother called.

"She sent her car and driver," Miranda says, indicating a man in blue serge slacks and short-sleeved shirt standing next to a maroon van parked near our white one. "So we won't all have to squeeze back into the school bus. Could you and Steve ride with Chet, Ivy and Sai in Chet's car?"

I recognize the van and the driver, who picks Chet up most afternoons. Everything about him, from his neat uniform to his immaculate vehicle to the careful way he buckles Chet into his car seat, instills confidence.

"Sure," I say, already luxuriating in the idea of a competent driver, an empty lap, and the relative quiet of just three kindergartners.

Steve and I buckle seatbelts around each of our charges as the driver watches in the rearview mirror.

Sai and Ivy are already asleep, or nearly so, when the driver turns around to whisper, "Ready for takeoff?" He waits for Chet to give him two thumbs up before starting the engine.

On our ride home, I wonder. Why didn't we have a big enough bus this morning? Did someone miscount? How hard was it for Chet's mom to send her driver to the museum? I'll never know. Like so much that happens at school, these questions are way AOPG.

But one question I *can* answer is this. Should I have spoken up in the white van? Yes. The children's safety should have been my main concern, but I used AOPG as an excuse to keep quiet.

As Chet dozes off, peace restored to his angelic face, I think about his mother, and all the other mothers and fathers and grandparents. I'd like to tell them, "I'm sorry. I won't let them take your sunshine away again."

Teacher, Mother, Mentor, Other

"Teacher Dian, I'm so nervous!" giggles Ling.

"Ling," I tease, "you know you can call me Dian." I probably should call her Laoshi Ling, because in Thailand everyone—students, parents, teachers, taxi drivers—uses a title to show respect to a teacher. At school I do so, but here in the dorm on a Sunday afternoon, the American in me balks at the formality.

Ling's tense smile shows the conflict between her respect for me and her affection. Respect not so much for my teaching prowess but simply because I'm older than her mother. Affection because, with her mother far away in China, Ling turns to me for support. Though she has abandoned our morning swim lessons—"So early, Teacher Dian!"—lately she has been visiting in the evening for help with her application to teach Chinese in the US. Having convinced Ling that her written application could be a smidge less self-effacing and two smidges more self-promoting, my goal today is to boost her self-confidence for her interview in Bangkok next weekend.

"Why don't you sit down?" I suggest. "More like a normal conversation."

"Oh, no," she insists. Ling wants this practice interview to be as realistic as possible. "I must stand, and you must sit." She must be sweltering in her black suit, stockings, and heels.

In my standard weekend attire, a loose-fitting faded denim

dress and bare feet, I sit up straighter, fold my hands in my lap, and clear my throat authoritatively for my role as senior Chinese interviewer.

"Laoshi Ling, your responses to my questions today will help us decide if you can be certified as a teacher of Chinese to Speakers of Other Languages and represent your country in America. First question: What is your greatest strength as a teacher?"

Ling beams and dives right in, explaining her core philosophy. "Children learn best when they are having fun." Singing, with hand signs and dance steps, she shows how she teaches the Chinese version of *It's a Small World*. I don't know if this qualifies her for a teaching post, but if Disneyland is recruiting, she's a shoo-in for a Mouseketeer job. She goes on to demonstrate teaching kids how to count in Chinese by playing hide-and-seek and how to greet people by playing with puppets. If her official interviewer gives points for bright eyes and cheery smiles, Ling will get full credit.

"All right," I reply. "Now let's imagine you are teaching in an American high school. Some students are not paying attention. Some are even sleeping at their desks. What would you do?"

Ling hesitates. Her already petite body visibly deflates. I wonder how she pictures the scene. Can she make the mental leap from kindergarten in Thailand, quite familiar territory, to high school in America, a whole new world? I inhale and exhale deeply, then roll my shoulders back, encouraging her to do the same.

Her tentative expression grows stern. "These children must leave the classroom and go to the school head," she pronounces. "They must not be disrespectful to their teacher." It's probably not what an American teacher would say, but maybe Ling's response would please the Chinese interviewer. I move on.

"Last question. What challenges do you expect to face in America?" Ling looks at me shyly, not wanting to offend. "Don't worry," I say. "Just answer honestly."

"Okay," she begins. "I am so excited to go to America. I really want to teach the Chinese language in your country. This is my dream.

"But I worry about American food, because it is not healthy. I like McDonald's, but it is not good to eat every day.

"And I worry about my mother. She was so sad when I left home to come to Thailand. It will be worse when I go to America."

Ling's words conjure thoughts of my own aged mother in America. When I asked for her thoughts on my plans to teach in Thailand, she skipped just a half-beat before giving her usual blessing, "*Gey gezunt.* Go. Have an adventure. I'll be fine here."

But I stay in surrogate interviewer role, thank Ling for her time, and say she will have her results next week. Then I switch to mentor mode, smile, and pat the red vinyl sofa cushion for her to sit beside me. She kicks off her heels and sighs.

"How do you think that went?" I ask.

"I think you asked hard questions."

"Which ones?"

"Well, I hope I won't have to talk about my mother."

"Mothers worry," I say. "All around the world. It's their job. But when you're ready to go to America, she'll support you, I'm sure." But am I?

I add, "Though I can't really put myself in her shoes."

Ling's gaze goes to her tiny black pumps on the floor, then to my bare feet. "Teacher Dian, I don't think you can wear my mother's shoes."

I laugh and switch roles again, to ESOL teacher. "Putting

yourself in someone else's shoes means experiencing the world the way they do."

Ling considers this, then wraps her arms around me and says, "I think you wear a mother's shoes very well."

Old Dogs Dine Out

In Pathum Thani, we don't cook. Our kitchen isn't equipped for any food preparation beyond our morning toast. Besides, we've reached a detente with the ants: if we don't cook, they won't invade.

Instead, we eat dinner out every evening, either sprinting across the highway to one of the half dozen roadside food stalls opposite our school or (when a break in the traffic seems like an impossible dream) taking a five-kilometer taxi ride to the local shopping center where we've become regulars at a few chain restaurants. After three months, this routine is growing stale, and in an effort to expand our culinary horizons, Steve searches the Internet.

"Hmm, this place looks promising," he says. "The Canal Café. Right here in Pathum Thani." The photos show a terrace at the water's edge, tiki torches in the gardens with strings of lights hanging from the trees, grilled fish dishes, and fruity icy drinks. Promising certainly. Maybe even enchanting. How could we have missed this place until now?

Our smartphone tells us to head west on the highway then turn left toward the canal. Simple. And close. We could probably walk the two kilometers, but since sidewalks along the highway are hit-or-miss, we opt for a taxi.

As we leave the dorm, the listless neighborhood mutt

Tarlo—we use his Thai name, even though our Filipina neighbors call him Jake, because he is a Thai dog, after all—vaguely lifts his ancient muzzle to note our departure, just as he does every evening at dinnertime. Little does Tarlo know that tonight is no ordinary night. Tonight we are up for adventure.

As always, it's only a few seconds before a cab pulls over. "*Raan ah haan* Canal Café *kha*," I tell the driver in my best Thai intonation. But, despite our weekly lessons with Khru Som, my best Thai intonation isn't much better than it was when we first arrived. I try the eight syllables again, more slowly and with more attention to what I think is a falling tone in the final syllable of the word for "restaurant." Still the driver is baffled. Steve tries a different tack and hands the driver his phone, displaying the route to the restaurant. After turning the phone around several times, the driver seems to understand our destination and waves us into his cab.

The map app works great on the highway, where it perfectly indicates where the heavy traffic is (everywhere) and when to make U-turns (frequently). But as soon as we turn into the side street, there is no correlation between the map, which suggests we go straight, and reality, which obliges us to make lefts and rights to stay near the canal. Worse, there seems to be no way to reach the little red dot on the screen, our destination, without driving through rice fields.

"Not far," our driver tells us, once, twice, and a third time as we penetrate deeper into darker, narrower streets.

Just as we're about to ask him to turn back, he spots a family sitting outside a small house. He stops and asks for the *raan ah haan*. I make a mental note of his pronunciation as they give him directions.

When we arrive, Steve pays the driver and I say, "*Sawaddee kha*" and wave goodbye—maybe not a brilliant move, as the place looks nothing like the photos Steve found online. It's an open-air roadside grill, just like the ones across from school. We look around, searching for twinkling lanterns and waterside gardens, though we'd be happy simply to find the cook.

"Wait here just a sec," Steve says. As he rounds the bend, a pair of dogs ambles up from the other direction. No collars, no tags, and not an ounce of spare flesh on their bones, these creatures make Tarlo look like a show dog. And they make me once again wish we had the rabies vaccine.

Slowly, I step back toward the grill for whatever protection it might offer. The dogs walk toward a nearby ice cooler and commence circling it. That's probably where the absent cook keeps provisions. For all I know, these dogs might well be regular customers here.

It's not a sec, but it's probably not more than a few minutes before Steve returns with good news. "I found it. The Canal Café. Come on."

Though the dogs follow us down the road, they stop when we reach the corner. Maybe they know they won't be welcome at the restaurant, which is as inviting in person as it is in pictures. Our table is on a canopied wooden pier. The canal is only a stone's throw wide, and the shamrock rice fields on the other side are darkening in the dimming twilight.

"This is more like it," Steve says. "Well worth the trip. What do you say we put the subject of dogs off-limits and enjoy our dinner?"

It's delicious, though perhaps mainly because we're celebrating simply having reached our destination. For dessert, we treat ourselves to blue sticky rice with coconut cream and mango. Then we ask our waiter for a taxi.

"Oh, taxis don't pass this way. But you can catch one by the highway," he says.

Can we walk out to the highway? It's not far, less than five hundred meters as the crow flies. But we aren't crows, it's dark out, and there's that pack of starving canines to consider.

For the first time in Thailand, we ask a ride-sharing app to come to our rescue. We wait. A long time. The driver sends a message that he is lost. The dot on Steve's phone screen shows he's on the other side of the highway. We cancel the request and place a new one. The second driver gets closer but can't seem to replicate the labyrinthine path we took to get here. We have no choice but to walk to the highway for a cab.

The route to the highway has neither sidewalks nor street-lights. We use our phones to light the way and keep to the middle of the road to avoid lurking animals. When we reach the highway, we are on the correct side, eastbound, but there is no sidewalk here either, so we have to take an underpass to the westbound side to hail a cab. Under the highway, we cautiously tiptoe past a grizzled dog lying in the gravel, but it seems too exhausted to bother with us.

Again, a taxi arrives quickly and within a few minutes drops us off at the school gate. Tarlo is there, just where we left him.

Tarlo is, theoretically, as free to wander about Pathum Thani as we are. But he always seems to be right here on the *soi* between the school and the apartments. As usual, he doesn't exactly greet us, just lifts his head off the asphalt to note our arrival.

"Do you think Tarlo has ever left this alley?" I ask Steve.

"Nah, not since Hector was a pup. I can't even imagine Tarlo as a pup." Tarlo cocks his head as if in protest. "Anyway," Steve adds, "now he knows better."

Steve and I aren't pups, and our days of throwing caution to the wind are behind us. But neither are we content to stay home and take life easy. We're in that stage of life, relatively new to our species, called active retirement. I don't know how a demographer or sociologist would define it, but I'd say it's a time when you're still willing (if, sensibly, somewhat hesitant) to go outside your comfort zone to do something worthwhile. The challenge is, you never know how far outside, or how worthwhile, until you give it a try.

Togetherness

Friday after school is our usual getaway time—taxi from Pathum Thani to the Lat Phrao Skytrain station (or, if the cabbie insists, the Mo Chit station), a weekend escape to Bangkok. Each trip, we explore different neighborhoods. We've figured out the river ferries and even have senior citizen passes for the subway. We have a favorite pizza place on Sukhumvit and are regulars at a nearby Thai massage studio. Some Sunday mornings, I take Howard's yoga class. We like to hang out at the Guggenheim-ish Bangkok Art and Culture Centre, both for the contemporary art exhibits and for the great café on the ground floor. But this weekend we'll have to make do with our instant Red Cup at home.

"I can't get upstairs without your help," Steve says, "let alone make it into the city." An hour ago, during classroom tidy-up time, Steve was scrubbing out some cubbies and somehow twisted his knee. Negotiating the hundred meters from school to the dorm, we looked more like conjoined twins than two separate people.

"Can you go to the Watsons and get an ice bag and a knee brace? And maybe a Snickers bar, too?" he asks.

Back home Steve is an avid, almost-daily runner. He's also an avid fan of Snickers, which is one of his main reasons for running—go for a run, burn calories, earn a candy bar. Or cookies, or ice cream, or all three.

Here in Pathum Thani, where the heat and lack of sidewalks or trails make running out of the question, he wears running shoes only for P.E. class on Wednesdays. To my mind, this is a good thing. This extended period of enforced rest might keep his knees—and hips and back and all his other joints—healthy, and forestall the pain and downtime of seemingly inevitable joint replacement surgeries. Pain and downtime not just for Steve, but for me, too.

His request for a brace means he's really hurting, though I know he won't say so. Unlike me, but rather like both our daughter Rose and our cat Minerva, Steve prefers to suffer in silence, to curl up under the covers and be left alone to heal. This suits me fine, since I'm not much for playing nursemaid. Luckily, or maybe because he's a fitness fanatic, he's never been seriously ill. As the years go by, and as friends and relatives deal with disease and decrepitude, I worry about how we'll cope when our time comes. Actually, I worry about how I'll cope, regardless of which of us is sick.

Five years ago, when a routine gynecological exam led to a diagnosis of thyroid cancer, a thyroidectomy, follow-up treatment, and no small measure of melodrama on my part, Steve rose to the challenge without complaint, just as he did twenty-two years earlier when a complicated pregnancy kept me on bed rest for four months. He came with me to doctor's appointments, monitored my meds, and prepared favorite meals, including vanilla tapioca pudding in Pyrex custard cups, just like my father used to make when either my sister or I was sick. Eventually, Steve did confiscate my little brass dinner bell, the one I've used (he'd say overused) since childhood to summon support during periods of recovery or confinement, but he never withheld my tapioca.

"Watson's? No problem," I say in a chipper tone, hiding my disappointment about our foiled plans to explore Bangkok's historic Chinatown, decked out for the upcoming Lunar New Year. "What else can I get you?" Steve doesn't want anything else, just to be left in peace to rest.

The drugstore is one of the few shops close to school. I'm always anxious when we walk there along the busy highway. Half of the route has a deteriorating sidewalk. Where there is no sidewalk, we are obliged to use the narrow shoulder of the road, where motorcyclists drive at top speed, often against the flow of traffic.

As I cautiously make my way, it dawns on me that I have never before walked this route alone. Not just that, but this is the first time I've been without Steve in Pathum Thani! In the four months we've been in Thailand, we've only spent a few hours apart, for a select few non-couple events in Bangkok like haircuts, yoga classes, and . . . and . . . oh my gosh, and nothing else! I can't think of three activities we've done flying solo!

Come next October, we'll have been married for thirty years, but we have never before accomplished such a marathon of togetherness. It would never have occurred to us even to try.

Steve and I met through work but then assiduously avoided any intersection of our professional careers. At first, I didn't want his reputation as an environmental policy expert to influence my budding research career. I was building my scientific "cred" (though I wouldn't have used that word at the time) on diligent analysis of atmospheric data, careful scrutiny of any conceivable data flaws, full disclosure of all known sources of uncertainty, and cautious caveats for all my conclusions about climate trends. I kept my maiden name for the first ten years of our marriage in part to avoid any accusation that my findings might be skewed to support Steve's regulatory objectives.

We're independent in our leisure lives, too. Steve is a runner; I practice yoga. I hate running; he hates yoga. We both love swimming, which is not exactly a social activity, but even so, at home we use different pools at different gyms. I gave up eating meat years ago; Steve relishes juicy hamburgers. We each have separate groups of friends who share our tastes and interests.

But now those people and pastimes are far away, and we teach in the same classroom every day. On weekends, we run errands, go shopping, and visit attractions as a duo. Evenings are quiet. After supper, together of course, we stay at home, stream episodes of *The Good Place* on a laptop, and go to bed early. Tonight, supper will have to be toast, or whatever junk food I find at Watson's. There's no way I'm crossing the highway alone during the evening rush hour to pick up a real dinner at a food stand.

Back at the dorm, I find Steve in bed, a pillow propped under his knee. "Here you go. Knee brace, ice bag."

"What, no Snickers?"

"Sorry, out of Snickers. Instead, I offer you Kisses." And I plant a wet one on his cheek. "Did you miss me?"

"I survived," he laughs. "Do you realize that was the first hour I've had to myself since we got here?"

"I do. We haven't had so much together time since our honeymoon. But that didn't last for four months!"

"Don't worry. We'll be back home soon enough," Steve says. "We'll get unglued. I promise."

"Unfortunately, you're not going home or anywhere else until that knee heals."

By Saturday morning, Steve's knee is already on the mend. We spend the weekend in Pathum Thani reading (historical biography for Steve, a novel for me) and polishing off the choc-olates, and by Monday he can walk without my support. He wears the knee brace to school and avoids scrubbing cubbies at tidy-up time.

On Wednesday, I teach Steve's P.E. class. Mainly, I follow the syllabus he's refined over the past few months—Simon Says, obstacle course, Red Light Green Light, relay races—but, for kicks and in the spirit of the season, I introduce Chinese jump rope. Miranda and Candace normally steer clear of P.E. class, but with Steve on injured reserve, they agree to help out when it becomes clear the kids can't stand still with the supersized rubber band around their ankles. While the kids have no trouble with the song—*I like coffee, I like tea, I'd like Ivy to jump with me*—they are skittish about the footwork and surprisingly hesitant to jump over the ropes.

Later, I'll wonder if the game spooked the children by con-juring the Thai superstition about stepping on door thresholds, but I'll never know. Woody Allen got it wrong—often, but particularly in his riff, "Those who can't do, teach. And those who can't teach, teach gym." Teaching gym takes talent, and the best-laid lesson plans often go awry. With Steve watching quietly from the sidelines—is that amusement or self-satisfaction in his smile?—Candace comes to my rescue.

"In South Africa, we call this elastics," she says. I take her place as rope holder as she launches into her chant, one I've never heard, and shows off her moves.

Next Miranda gives it a try. "We used bamboo sticks to play in the Philippines, but I like the rubber band!" she laughs as the steps of her childhood return to her. Enlisting Ivy's ankles to take my place, I join Miranda, and our little duet earns the enthusias-tic applause of the whole class.

"That was fun," gasps Miranda, doubled over, her hands on her knees.

"You're good!" I tell her. It *was* fun. As much fun as I've ever had with my coteachers.

"But exhausting!" She catches her breath and adds, "When I'm your age, I hope I have half as much energy as you and Teacher Steve."

Ouch. But I'll take it as the compliment she means it to be. I'm old, but not too old to jump rope. I look over to Steve on the bench. Today he's too old to jump, but I have faith that he'll be younger again in a day or two.

On Friday afternoon, Steve and I fill our backpacks with our usual gear—passports, laptops, swimsuits, goggles, toiletries, water bottles, and one change of clothes.

"You should take the ice bag and knee brace," I tell him.

"I'm perfectly capable of packing my bags," he answers, "all by myself." The boys in K1 and K2 never reject my assistance, though I often wish they would. Getting a teacher's help generally beats doing something "all by myself" in their world. But my husband isn't interested in being coddled and never has been. I'm hoping he'll stay that way for a long time to come. But, just in case, I tuck the bag and brace into the secret compartment of my backpack.

Leap Years

"Jump!" Ivy commands. "You can do it!" she urges Sai and Chompoo, who are peering down at her from the jungle gym's highest platform. Only Ivy, the oldest and tallest girl at school, jumps from such a height, her black braids flying behind her. My approach to playground duty is to keep watch from the shade of a frangipani tree and interfere only if injury seems imminent. I scolded Ivy the first time she jumped, but I don't anymore. She can't resist the thrill, and she always sticks her landing. Besides, I like that Ivy does something none of the boys do.

Decades ago and a world away, I liked Cheryl's daring feats on the playground, too. The sugar-maple-dappled sunlight catching her glorious red hair, Cheryl could hang from her knees on the monkey bars, shimmy up the tetherball pole, and fly off the swings to stick her own landing on the brittle, late-autumn grass. In our third-grade threesome, I was older and taller than Susie and Cheryl, but Cheryl was the undisputed alpha girl.

Here in Pathum Thani, Ivy generates the same magnetic magic for the girl gang. Dreamy Sai and attentive Chompoo happily let Ivy lead them by the hand and organize their play. It's sweet watching their friendship grow, but Ivy's "Jump!" presents a new wrinkle. Is it a big-sisterly bit of encouragement or a dangerous dare? How will the younger girls take her challenge? How will I?

Swinging between Susie and me, Cheryl was already flying highest when she called out, "Higher!" We took her challenge. We synced our legs, pumped harder, and rose higher . . . until my head, or maybe my stomach, started to spin. To regain solid ground, I dragged the tips of my saddle shoes in the grass, slowed my swing, and dismounted. But loyal Susie sailed on, higher still. "Come on! Let's jump!" shouted Cheryl. I don't know what Susie heard. Encouragement? Dare? I heard only derision, directed at me, as I watched from below. Then Cheryl called out, "You and me on three!" Susie didn't wait for the count. My stomach did another flip at the sight of Susie, fearless, flying through the air.

Sai calls down to Ivy, "I'm coming." Where has Sai, the timid girl, the girl like me, found the courage to jump? She won't, she can't, stick this landing. I run and reach the jungle gym just in time to see Sai's round-toed Mary Janes emerge from the bottom of the tube slide. The girl like me is right where she belongs— not in flight but standing solidly, safely, on the ground.

Maybe Chompoo can stick the landing. She is younger now than Susie was then but just as fearless, and I don't want to introduce her to the anxious self-doubt that I've carried since childhood. I look her in the eyes, smile, nod, and whisper, "Jump!"

When Susie returned to school, we signed her cast with Magic Markers. But Susie's face made clear that, for her, the magic was gone. It was gone for me, too. Our threesome didn't survive Susie's absence from the playground, and the hard work of finding new friends lay ahead.

"Good girl," I tell Chompoo, as I catch her capable little body and give her a quick hug.

Someday, this threesome might also dissolve. Someday, someone might get hurt. But today, each girl is happy, each her own self. To the playground gods I pray: Let their bodies survive and their friendship thrive, at least while I'm here. Let these girls make or break the magic on someone else's watch.

Sojourners

A breakwater of boulders, maybe five meters wide and extending fifty meters into the teal water of the Gulf of Thailand, is all that separates the fishing shack from our carefully raked beach, with its tidily aligned, umbrella-shaded chaise longues, each with two jelly rolls of white Turkish towel. The snout-prow dinghy that I noticed yesterday—who could miss it, with its painted wooden hull striped pink, green, and orange?—is gone this morning. With the fishers away, perhaps netting tonight's feast, the other side of the breakwater beckons.

When Steve booked this Koh Samui resort for our rendezvous with Rose, he told me, "You're gonna hate it. It's completely over-the-top." A pause, a chortle. "You're gonna love it!"

We've had that conversation many times over the years. Our vacations are mostly visits to Steve's boyhood home at the Jersey shore, where we cook our own meals, make our own beds, schlep our own rusty beach chairs, use the same faded beach towels he used as a child, and schmooze with his relatives.

But on those rare occasions when we vacation elsewhere, Steve likes luxury. Four stars minimum, five stars preferred. I balk at the exorbitant room rates, the fancy toiletries in tiny plastic bottles that I'm sure won't be recycled, the AC that's always on full blast when you open your door even though you turned it off when you left, the fresh towels that arrive even when you dutifully hang damp ones up to reuse, and a hundred other extravagances. But as he says, I may complain, but somehow I manage to tolerate the million-thread-count Egyptian cotton sheets, stunning swimming pools, and warm chocolate chip cookies at bedtime.

Of Thailand's 1,430 islands, we picked Koh Samui because there are direct flights from Bangkok for us, and from Chiang Mai for Rose. Before starting her final semester of grad school, and before getting married, she's here on vacation. Last week youth hosteling and hiking on her own in northern Thailand, this weekend at the beach with us. Next week onward to parts unknown.

"Not too shabby," she said when the resort van delivered us to our villa. "Dad picked it, I presume?"

The fruit bowl on the sleek teak table was photo-worthy, as is every decorative detail. Removing a rambutan and ruining the architecture of the arrangement, I offered it to Rose.

"Try this. You'll love it," I said. With their ruby-red husks covered in barbed spikes, I adore these little milk-colored yum-drops whose spicy floral flavor might well have been the inspiration for Juicy Fruit gum. Rambutans aren't in season, and we've only seen them once in a market at a ridiculous price, but as eye candy they can't be beat.

Our perch on the cliffside has a bird's-eye view of the beach, where the white swags of a canopy billow in the sea breeze.

"Pretty place for a wedding," I said.

"For somebody, maybe. Not for us," Rose said, and I was relieved that she isn't dreaming of an over-the-top destination wedding. She'll find a venue that's convenient for family and friends.

My beach read is Alex Garland's cult novel *The Beach*, set

here on the east side of the Malay Peninsula, the elephant's trunk on the map of Thailand. This quote intrigues me: ". . . tourists went on holidays while travellers did something else. They *travelled.*"

In the book, the young *farangs* set out with rucksacks and a secret map in search of an unspoiled island paradise. They hire a local spiv (that's British slang for a shady character) to take them by boat from Koh Samui to a smaller island nearby. If the rucksacks and the spiv aren't enough to make them travelers, surely forsaking most of their belongings and swimming over open water to the secret island is.

What are Steve and I—tourists or travelers? We've been living in Pathum Thani for four months now, but it's not home. Home is Maryland, and there's no doubt that we'll be returning there in March.

I don't think we are expats, though the word is a tricky one, especially when you try to distinguish it from migrant, guest worker, immigrant, or refugee. In my mind, expats in Thailand are *farangs* who live, work, and play primarily with other *farangs*. That's not us.

On weekends, you might call us tourists. We're certainly doing our best to hit all the recommended tourist sites in Pathum Thani, Bangkok, and nearby provinces, but when asked, we don't say we're tourists. We say we are teachers, and we say it in Thai.

Maybe you could call us sojourners. I like the biblical connotation—outsiders staying for a while, maybe a long while, in a strange land and depending on the goodwill of strangers. But if we are sojourners in Pathum Thani, here in Koh Samui we are indisputably tourists.

After breakfast—the expansive international buffet Steve and I have come to expect at high-end hotels in Thailand—Steve and Rose set out toward an island that might have inspired *The Beach*. They aren't swimming. They are going tourist style, on a swanky speedboat with a captain and two mates who will help them with their snorkeling gear, give them a guided tour of the local marine life, and serve refreshments as they motor back to our beach.

With half a day to myself, I swim along the beach, back and forth for three laps, then put on my sunhat and make my way over the boulders.

The roof and walls of the ramshackle fishing hut on the other side of the breakwater are an assemblage of fallen fronds from nearby palm trees. Under a patch of shade are two low stools, the stackable plastic kind on which Bangkok street-food customers squat-sit to eat. A faded blue T-shirt is draped over a makeshift clothesline strung between two palms. It all has an air of impermanence, until I notice the spirit house.

Spirit houses, and spirits, are everywhere in Thailand, and Thai people take good care of both. Most of the spirit houses we've seen in central Thailand are intricately carved, colorfully painted, gold-trimmed structures mounted on a post or pedestal. This one is different, a miniature version of the fishing shack, but arranged under the roof is the usual sort of offering: a little bowl of rice, a magenta bloom I can't identify, and an open bottle of strawberry Fanta, complete with straw. I've come to expect Fanta, or an equally red Thai brand. I hope the local spirits find it as endearing as I do, bring the fishers good luck today, and maybe watch over Steve and Rose, too.

"Madam," I hear a voice behind me say. "May I help you?"

The slender young man in the resort's uniform—khaki shorts and white polo shirt—is smiling. But which of the thirteen varieties of Thai smile is this? Probably one that means, "You really shouldn't be here, but you're a hotel guest, so rather than cause you to lose face, I'll escort you back where you belong." And, if the wandering tourist seems disgruntled, maybe it'll also mean, "I'll even offer you a piña colada to sweeten the deal."

But I'm not disgruntled. I know that the tourists belong on the other side of the breakwater. I offer him a *khop khun kha*, with my best intonation, that I hope tells him I'm not always a tourist.

"Your family will return from snorkeling soon," he says as we walk back to the beach. His familiarity with our plans is impressive and meant to make guests feel special. He probably knows our hometown, how we take our coffee, and which DVDs we borrowed from the front desk. But the lack of privacy is another feature of fancy resorts that sets my teeth on edge. As if on cue, I hear the *brr-brr-brr* of the speedboat as it comes into view.

By evening, chairs and linen-topped tables have magically appeared on the beach. Rose and Steve, their sunburned faces glowing in the twinkly lights strung from palm to palm, are refreshed, having napped the late afternoon away. They're still gushing about the snorkeling.

Steve is mildly amused by my excursion to the cove next door.

"Exploring the neighborhood?" he asks, using a family euphemism. J. R. R. Tolkien wrote, "Not all those who wander are lost," but when I'm the one wandering, or exploring the neighborhood, getting lost is part of the adventure.

"No," I say. "You can't get lost on a beach."

I order the catch of the day. "Excellent choice," the waiter says. "Delicate white filet, mild flavor. As fresh as can be," he assures us. I guess the spirits were pleased with the Fanta and flowers.

I love that Rose roams the world with confidence, whether as tourist or traveler. But I hope someday she and her husband will live and work abroad and be neither tourist nor traveler. Whatever you call what Steve and I are doing, and whether or not it's the path we had hoped to take, it's been an adventure. And we are not lost.

An Opening

The barista's face brightens when we open the sliding glass door. It must be lonely working the evening shift at Café Noah, where we've yet to see another customer. Steve and I would be happy to give the coffee shop, across the highway from our dorm, more business. We've stopped by many times after supper seeking air conditioning and a change of scenery as much as iced coffee and mango cake, but more often than not the lights are out. This evening, we are in luck. We are reading and nursing our drinks as we nestle into the café's overstuffed armchairs (which could win a Most Comfortable Chair in Pathum Thani contest, hands down).

"Whoa!" Steve says, as the café door opens, letting in a mass of warm, moist air. "Look who's here!"

Miranda? She often stays a little late at school, waiting for a few of the teachers from the *rong rian* to share a cab to their apartments, a few kilometers down the highway. But it's well after dark now, and she's alone.

"And look who's here," Miranda says, with only a sliver of her usual cheer. She heads straight to the counter to order, then to the restroom, before joining us.

"Miranda, what's up?" I ask after she slumps into the sofa. "Have you been at school all evening?"

She nods as the barista brings her drink, an enormous

concoction that's more ice cream soda than coffee.

"Dinner?" I ask.

She nods again, smiles weakly, sighs, and scoops a spoonful of whipped cream into her mouth. She squeezes her eyes shut, holds her breath, and lets out a muffled whimper.

"I shouldn't do it," she says.

"Do what?" I say, placing a hand on her shoulder.

Another scoop of whipped cream. A long sip through her extra long straw.

"I filled out a job application. . . . But I shouldn't send it." A friend from her Montessori training program teaches at a school in Ho Chi Minh City, and they are hiring.

"And you want to go?" Steve asks.

"They told me I'd have a real Montessori class, all day long. Not just the hour each day I have here," Miranda says.

"Sounds right up your alley," I say. "So what's holding you back?"

Miranda hesitates, then says, "It wouldn't be right to leave Prep. I started the Montessori program here. I've known our kids since they were two years old. They're like family."

Now I put both my hands on her shoulders and look her in the eyes.

"Miranda, your loyalty to Prep is admirable. But you need to be more loyal to yourself. What do *you* want?"

"I know, I know," she says and takes another long swig. "But I don't know. I *really* don't know."

"Doors like this don't open often. At least, in my experience," I say.

Three times doors like this—invitations to work with colleagues in England, Spain, and Israel—opened for me in my career. But I didn't walk through. Now my options for working abroad are much more limited. I'd like to tell Miranda, but then she'd ask why I didn't go. There's no need to tell her that nobody encouraged me to pull up stakes, take a risk, try something new. No need to explain that the only people I asked for advice were family members and that I let their preferences take precedence. Anyway, the ties that bind Miranda are different from mine.

"When's the application due?" Steve, always the practical one, asks.

"Midnight," Miranda whispers.

"Listen," I say, "you can apply now and make up your mind later. But if you miss the deadline, you're closing the door before you even see what's behind it. Go home. Send it. You don't want to wake up tomorrow with regrets."

She nods slowly. We finish our drinks, tell the barista good night, and walk out together into the muggy evening. We hail a taxi, and before Miranda gets in, she hugs first Steve, then me. It's a hug like I haven't felt in a long time, Miranda's exhalations melting her body into mine.

"Go home. Send the application. Then get some rest. We'll talk tomorrow," I say before closing the taxi door.

When we talk tomorrow, she'll have taken only one of my suggestions. Maybe another door, maybe two, will open for Miranda somewhere down the road, and maybe she'll have the fortitude to cross the threshold. Or maybe she won't. Maybe, like me, she'll make other people her priority. Doing that takes fortitude, too.

Keep Calm and Wash Your Hands

The last message from the US Embassy in Bangkok encouraged us to be good citizens and vote in the upcoming primary elections. You bet we will. Today's message isn't nearly as upbeat, and it's not at all clear what we should do.

The US Centers for Disease Control and Prevention reports that a novel coronavirus is causing an outbreak of respiratory illness in China. As of late January 2020, five cases have been detected in Thailand. The health alert recommends these four actions:

- *Avoid all nonessential travel to Wuhan, China.*
- *Wash hands often with soap and water for at least 20 seconds. Use an alcohol-based hand sanitizer if soap and water are not available.*
- *Cover your mouth and nose with a tissue or your sleeve (not your hands) when coughing or sneezing.*
- *If you traveled to Wuhan and feel sick, or were exposed to someone who was in Wuhan in the last six weeks who has fever, cough, or difficulty breathing, seek medical care right away.*

"Should we share this with the other teachers?" I ask Steve.

"No need to get them worried. We're a long way from Wuhan," he says.

"But how about all this personal hygiene advice? The kids

could certainly learn a thing or two about germs, don't you think?" After some discussion, we agree that a class on viruses and bacteria would be well above grade level for our students, but that, novel virus or not, their hand-washing skills and sneeze hygiene could stand an upgrade.

"Isn't hygiene usually the P.E. teacher's domain?" I ask. Steve's Wednesday outdoor P.E. sessions are the highlights of his workweek and the only class that reliably keeps the most rambunctious kids fully engaged.

He balks, and I add, "Didn't your junior high gym teacher give you the talk about our changing bodies?" Apparently not. Steve is seven years older than me, and the sexual revolution happened between his years in junior high school and mine. For him, gym class meant dodgeball and jumping jacks, not hormones and body hair.

Mostly, though, he just doesn't want to relinquish any of his precious P.E. class time. We compromise and agree to share this self-imposed teaching assignment during other parts of the school day.

I opt for story time and take a musical tack. Sitting on the floor on the orange circle, our story time gathering point, I sing, "This is the way we wash our hands, wash our hands, wash our hands . . . " and, without water, demonstrate how to wash the fronts and backs, between the fingers, and even the thumbs.

It doesn't take long for the kids to learn the song and to suggest times besides *so early in the morning* for their own scrubbing up. *Before we eat our breakfast. After we use the toilet.* And for reasons I don't fully understand, and elect not to investigate, *when we wake up from our nap.*

"Well done," I say. And I mean it. Unlike most of my other lessons, this one has captivated the children, who are fascinated with their own and their friends' little hands.

Not willing to rest on these laurels, I say, "Now let's try with soap and water." Six kindergartners stand at the knee-high trough sink, sing two verses (for the recommended twenty seconds), and have a grand old time before the second group gets its turn. Despite the puddles on the floor and soaked uniforms, I consider this lesson a success.

Steve's sneezing lesson poses more of a challenge. The kids wear short-sleeved uniform shirts, so sneezes will have to be aimed at bare inner elbows. When they have runny noses, they come to school with cotton handkerchiefs buttoned to their shirts and run around all day with the germ-ridden banners flying in the breeze. We don't have lots of tissues, toilet paper, or paper towels at school, because they clog the delicate Thai plumbing systems. Which is why we all spray ourselves clean with bum guns after using the toilet. If you can imagine how well two-, three-, and four-year-olds manage this, you understand why the drenching during the hand-washing lesson didn't faze me.

Steve opts to take his sneezing lesson outdoors where he can keep the kids several arms' distance apart. First he demonstrates, then he gives instructions. "Simon says sneeze in your elbow. Simon says cough on your arm." Everyone does as Simon says, until they hear the command, "Sneeze in my face," which the kids find hilarious.

They get the message. Good for them, and good for all of us. Now we just have to teach them how to laugh safely. What advice might the embassy have to offer about that? We'll just have to hope that this novel coronavirus doesn't reach our little corner of the world, because stifling children's laughter in the name of public health seems the saddest policy imaginable.

The Buddha of My Dreams

"It was a wedding. Maybe our wedding? Maybe Rose's?" I'm speaking fast, to tell Steve about the dream before the images vanish into the predawn darkness. "You were in a wooden chair, held up in the air, and golden Buddhas were circle-dancing around you."

"Sounds like a nightmare to me," Steve mutters, rolling toward his side of the bed. "Go back to sleep."

"No, this means something. How often do I remember dreams? Help me out here."

Steve sighs and says, "What happened next?"

"I woke up. To a clarinet playing *Hava Nagila*. What do you think it means?"

"It means you're obsessing over our daughter's wedding. And you've been spending too much time staring at Buddhas. Now let me sleep."

Steve's dismissive analysis prompts an equally dismissive snort. His first point is plain wrong. Rose's wedding is more than a year away. I'm not obsessing about it nor will I . . . at least until we return home.

The second is too obvious. With just over a month left before we leave, we are trying to see all the top sights in Pathum Thani province, most of which are Buddhist temples. Yesterday we visited Wat Phra Dhammakaya, Thailand's largest *wat*.

"On the dome are three hundred thousand seated Buddha figures covered in gold leaf," recited the guide as we trained binoculars on the temple a kilometer away. The Buddhas dazzled in the reddening late-day light. "Inside are seven hundred thousand more."

A million identical Buddhas, arranged in perfect concentric circles. I couldn't fathom it. Whoever designed the temple and the vast open spaces that surround it must have been dreaming of the power of large numbers. Meditating together in multitudes is said to bring people closer to one another and closer to the divine. I can't quite fathom that, either.

Some people come to Thailand to find their Buddha nature. They go to temples and meditate with the monks. Not me. I would be happy simply to have found a Thai friend.

We get along fine with the teachers at school, but they aren't Thai and we rarely see them outside school hours. Our students' parents and grandparents shower us with gifts and gratitude, but none has ever included us in a social event. Our relationship with Dr. Pat and the General is warm enough, but it is so steeped in mysteries that I'm always tentative when we're together. The Buddhas in my dream are a sign that we have acquaintances but no true friends in Thailand.

Buddha images have two salient, and somewhat unsettling, attributes: perfect posture that always makes me correct my own and meditative eyes focused either inward or far away, but never at you. My dream Buddhas are different. They have personality, great dance moves, and no basis in reality. They symbolize neither a spiritual community nor a social group. Maybe if I had focused on cultivating friendships instead of touring around Pathum Thani—and neighboring Bangkok, Nonthaburi, and Ayutthaya—my dreams would be populated by real people rather than gold-robed Buddhas.

That's the interpretation I give Steve when he finally wakes up. He shakes his head in disbelief. "Here you are, dreaming of dancing Buddhas—which, I admit, is pretty cool—and you turn it into a pity party about not having Thai friends?" In his words, I hear my lifelong struggle to find friendship surfacing. Tears drip to my pillow.

"You're not alone here, you know," he says more gently. "If you were, it would be a different story. You'd surely have made friends. By necessity.

"We spend our days with the children," he continues. "They are our little buddies, the people we've come to know best, and the ones we'll remember best when we leave. We don't have adult friends because we have each other. People don't invite us places because they know we're together."

Steve's right, of course. I do have dreams of a wedding and of rejoicing and reconnecting with family and friends when we return home. And if I were here alone, I probably would have a new friend or two. But, given the choice, I'd much rather be here with Steve. I'd much rather wake up in the middle of the night, dreaming of dancing golden Buddhas, next to my best friend in Thailand.

A Crown for the Year of the Rat

"Teacher Dian, I'm sorry to bother you, but I need your advice," Miranda says. I've worked in her classroom for four months now, and this is the first time she's phoned. It's not the first time she has asked my advice, but those other occasions were spontaneous, coming at the end of a frustrating school day when some nonsense from a parent or from the school has made Miranda reconsider her career options. I've gently encouraged her to expand her horizons, but it's clear she's not ready. Without some formidable external force, her love for the Prep kids and loyalty to the school will keep her in Pathum Thani.

It's hard to imagine why she's calling now, on a Sunday evening, but maybe it has something to do with the messages that have been flurrying online among the parents over the past few days. Because they have all been in Thai, some with attached newspaper articles and other documents, I've assumed they weren't relevant to me. Apparently, I've assumed wrong.

"Chompoo's mother doesn't think Panit should come back to school tomorrow," she begins. Odd. We rarely get complaints from Chompoo's parents, who seem thrilled with their precocious two-year-old's growing self-confidence and English proficiency. Last week, with her rambunctious friend Panit on vacation (giving us teachers a vacation from chasing after him), Chompoo asked daily, "When is Panit coming back?"

"Because of the virus," Miranda continues. "Some other parents don't want him back in school yet, either. But Panit's mother says he's healthy and he misses school." Dissension among the parents—difficult for any teacher, but a special problem in Thailand, where conflict avoidance is a high art, and a special problem for Miranda. She speaks Thai well enough to manage daily life (a major achievement in my book), but not well enough for diplomatic negotiations with young mothers. And she wants *my* advice?

A week ago, Panit and his family traveled to China to welcome the Year of the Rat with Panit's grandparents. At the same time, media reports of the novel coronavirus spreading in China were becoming more urgent, and the first cases outside China were detected in Bangkok.

Panit's last day in class was our school's own Lunar New Year celebration, orchestrated by Laoshi Ling, who taught a special song, *Gong xi, gong xi, gong xi ni*. Of course, she taught an accompanying dance with hand gestures, as much to release surplus youthful energy as to reinforce the lyrics about the end of winter and coming of spring. The class photo Miranda sent to the parents that afternoon was a keeper, with all the kids and all the teachers in our reddest outfits for good luck in the new year.

All except Panit, who was resplendent in a suit of gold silk brocade, his perfectly round face and his jet-black bowl-cut hair crowned in a matching gold cap. Under his jacket, I'm sure he was wearing his burnished brass amulet on a chain around his neck.

Panit is the only student who wears an amulet. I've tried asking him what it means, but he sees it mainly as something to put in his mouth. Amulets like his are sold at temples. They're supposed to have protective powers or bring good luck. I hope

Panit's worked its magic during his stay in China.

Like many of Panit's glorious outfits, his golden suit didn't survive the school day. It's hard to keep party clothes clean while filling, frying, dipping, and devouring pork dumplings, our festive addition to the school lunch menu.

"What does Dr. Pat think?" I ask. Miranda can't read Thai, but surely she's been in touch with Dr. Pat about the online messages. And surely resolving this dispute is above Miranda's pay grade.

"She thinks Panit shouldn't be in the classroom," Miranda explains. Relieved, I exhale. Dr. Pat, who has been a school director for thirty or forty years, can handle a delicate situation.

But Miranda continues. "She wants you to stay with him in the office and teach him separately. For two weeks—like a quarantine."

I picture myself confined all day in a small office with a child who loves nothing more than running around the playground at top speed pushing a wheelbarrow full of stones, who resists being picked up and placed in a chair with the muscular determination of a Thai water buffalo, and who might have been exposed to a lethal respiratory disease. It's lucky that Miranda can't see my face and that she can interpret my speechlessness as something more measured than the outrage I'm feeling.

"I told her I would phone you," she says. "Is this a good idea?"

It doesn't take much for her to agree that it is not. After all, if Panit is infected, and if he infects me, I'll infect Steve, who will in turn infect the rest of the class, some of whom have siblings at the *rong rian* where several hundred kids and their teachers could be exposed.

We also agree that a good idea would be for me to speak

with Dr. Pat directly—as one sixtysomething-year-old woman to another. I am counting on Dr. Pat's friendship and a healthy dose of Thai confrontation avoidance to pave the way.

"You're calling about Panit and the wireless?" Dr. Pat asks as soon as she hears my voice. Ah, a five-letter English word with two nightmare letters for a Thai speaker.

"Yes, Panit and the virus." And I hardly have to say anything more.

"You don't want to have him in the office? I understand," she says. Maybe Dr. Pat just needed to see the situation through my eyes. "He can stay home. Please tell Teacher Miranda."

I call Miranda right away. My problem is solved, but she still has to deal with the parents. I offer to draft a message proclaiming our love for Panit, invoking Dr. Pat's concern for all the students, and using terms like "current medical advice," "precautionary measure," and, most pointedly, "fourteen-day home quarantine."

Panit's quarantine should end on a Monday. But that particular Monday is the full moon of the third month of the Thai lunar calendar—the national Makha Bucha holiday. This celebration of a historic, apparently unannounced, assembly of the Buddha's first 1,250 disciples is a day of merit-making in Thailand, and schools are closed.

That Monday also happens to be my sixty-first birthday. We leave Panit, Miranda, Dr. Pat, and all thoughts of school in Pathum Thani and head to Bangkok for the long weekend.

There—in the Italian restaurant, at the hotel swimming pool, and on the crowded streets and subway trains—we expose ourselves to many more than 1,250 Chinese tourists, whose free access to the city and its people the Thai government has not yet restricted. It will be a month before the words *pandemic* and *social distancing* dominate our collective vocabulary, and this weekend in Bangkok is not much different from the ones before.

Tuesday morning, after three weeks away from school, Panit arrives in his school uniform, his amulet around his neck. No golden crown, no coronavirus. Just a sweet, shy smile for his teacher, who picks him up for a welcome-back hug.

"We've missed you, Panit," I tell him, as his mother looks on at the school gate.

I'm not being completely honest. It's been delightfully peaceful in K1 without Panit. And I'm looking forward to the day, less than a month away, when I'll say goodbye to Pathum Thani Prep and all its craziness.

But I'm not lying, either. Though teaching tiny tots was not what I had envisioned for my overseas experience, I've grown to love them all. And I wish them all good luck in the Year of the Rat. Little do I realize how much we're all going to need it.

Inspiration and Exhalation

Some sit, some stand, some recline, and some walk. There's a different Buddha posture for each day of the week. According to Thai custom, because I was born on a Tuesday, I should be drawn to the reclining Buddha. He rests on his right side, right hand propping up his head, in his final moments before entering Nirvana. The concept seems heavenly, but that neck position looks painful, and those stylized Tuesday Buddhas don't inspire me. The Thursday Buddha, seated in lotus pose—now that's another story.

Seated Buddhas are everywhere in Thailand. Their hand gestures, robes, and facial features vary, but they all sit cross-legged with one or both feet resting on the opposite thigh. My favorite is in Pak Kret, not far from Pathum Thani. On the left bank of the camo-colored Chao Phraya River, the gleaming gilded Buddha rises eight stories into the ever-hazy Thai sky. The legs are like a floating lotus leaf, and the straight spine ascends stemlike to support the perfectly balanced head. In such a pose, a moment of meditative silence, a blossoming of the spirit, a connection with what some call the divine seems possible. I've been working on lotus pose for months.

The Pak Kret Buddha could be my inspiration, but in practice it's the children. Kids everywhere are flexible, but from my first day at Pathum Thani Prep I've marveled at how effortlessly

Thai kids pretzel their legs in a single plane perfectly parallel to the floor. A few kids in our class go more naturally into W-sitting, kneeling with their hypermobile hips between their feet, knees wide, feet splayed. But most, like Chet, prefer lotus.

Chet is a sensitive child. Chet is the one who stops running with the rest of the boy-pack to comfort the classmate who trips on the playground. His is the sole vote against reading *Chicken Licken* at story time. He knows that (in our school's edition, pre-dating trigger warnings) Foxy Loxy is very bad news for Ducky Lucky, Goosey Loosey, and Chicken Licken's other avian friends. At home, I might call Chet an old soul. Here I phrase it differently: Chet is closer to his Buddha nature than the rest of us.

I keep Chet and the Pak Kret Buddha in mind each morning as I work on lotus pose. But with signs of arthritis in my hips, knees, ankles, and heck, even my toes, I approach with caution. I prepare with other poses and save lotus for the end of my practice. On good days, I can stay for a few breaths. Focusing on inhalations and exhalations makes the posture tolerable, though not even marginally meditative. Then I carefully unwind.

I usually do yoga before sunrise, but even then our living room is hot, so I practice in a swimsuit and head straight to the school pool afterward. It's the best moment of the day. My joints welcome the cool water and the fluid movements of my flutter kick. The rhythm of my breath is relaxed and easy. I don't have to think. My body knows exactly what to do, lap after lap.

The Buddha sits in lotus pose to meditate. When Chet and the other boys at school are older and ordain as monks for a few weeks or months, as most young men in Thailand do, I imagine they will sit to meditate, too. Maybe when they are my age, they'll still be sitting in lotus. I'll work on the pose while I'm here, with Chet and the Buddha as inspiration, but how long will my old joints put up with this effort?

Over the past twenty years I've devoted a lot of time to yoga, but over the course of this sixty-plus-year incarnation I've spent many more hours in the water than on a mat. I feel at home in the water. Nothing hurts in the water.

On dry land things do hurt, and they remind me of my own mortality. I'd like to think that I have an equanimous outlook on the subject. My mother seems to face the prospect with admirable acceptance. Still, she has long hoped for a peaceful death. "I just want to go to sleep one night and not wake up in the morning," she's said more than a few times. Though I don't like to hear her talk about it, her plan appeals to me, too. But I've got a more specific wish.

On the day I lay me down to rest for the last time, I'd like to have done a little yoga and gone for a swim. And if I can't die in my sleep, maybe I could die in the ocean, swept under by a wave.

If I were a better student of meditation, I'd let go of these thoughts of death and Chet and Buddhas. I'd clear my mind and find an inner peace. But my mind pays attention to my body, ever more so as I get older. We'll see whether yoga or swimming or anything else will carry me through to my final exhalation.

Our Peeps

The octopus's green eye gazes at us benevolently as its orange, red, and turquoise arms curlicue around the room and almost embrace us. This photo of our farewell dinner in Pathum Thani will be a keeper. I adore that gigantic cephalopod in the mural, and I love the smiles on everyone's faces. These are our peeps, the half dozen teachers we've come to know best—Miranda, Candace, Ting, Ling, Nok, and Som.

We've already said our goodbyes to Dr. Pat, who is out of town today. She and the General are planning a family vacation to America in November, and although that's eight months away I already have ideas for sightseeing tours and menus. Tonight's menu, however, is beyond my control.

"How about the pineapple fried rice?" Steve says. The dish is an eye-catching, chili-free presentation of shrimp, chicken, and curried rice in a pineapple boat. After spotting it on another party's table, Steve ordered it the first time we ate here. Pineapple fried rice and that glorious octopus on the wall are the reasons we're back tonight.

"*Khao pad sapparod,*" I tell Khru Som.

"*Khao pad sapparod,*" she says with a smile and with a completely different musicality. She says it three times and I dutifully repeat, just as we've been doing in our weekly language lessons.

"OK. But tonight you'll try some new foods," Khru Som

says. She and Khru Nok have a lengthy consultation with the server. The other six of us, from four different countries, gladly defer to the locals and enjoy the rare, stress-free restaurant order. The dishes arrive one by one in a steady stream. Some are off-limits for the chili-intolerant Chinese and Americans, but there are plenty of *mai ped* choices. We've never eaten so well in Pathum Thani.

And we've never eaten so companionably in Pathum Thani, unless you'd characterize supervising fourteen under-five-year-olds as companionship. This counts as a real dinner party. The lively conversation and warm sense of togetherness around the table won't be undone by sentimental speeches or teary hugs, since we'll see everyone again tomorrow, our last day at school.

No one arranged it, but we are all in pairs in the photo. Steve stands next to me, and Khru Som stands next to Khru Nok, whose stunning smile is the focal point of the picture. Candace and Miranda, who will have a new teacher in their classroom next week, have their arms around each other's shoulders in solidarity. Ling and Ting are making little "I love you" hearts with their thumbs and forefingers. They'll be returning to China a few weeks after we leave, and our imminent departure is making them giddy for their own.

After dinner, the group presents us a gift: dark blue Hmong-style jackets with hand-stitched embroidery and quilt work.

"Khru Nok chose them especially for you," says Miranda.

"What would we wear without you, Khru Nok?" Steve says. "I remember our first day in Pathum Thani, when you sent us our uniforms. We've been wearing them almost every day since." Once bright orange, our polo shirts are now stained and faded to a shade of bruised melon.

"You can wear these tomorrow, your last Traditional Thai

Dress Day," Khru Nok says with a wink.

Though we've tried to fit in at school, we've failed to get with the Traditional Thai Dress program. On Fridays, no one wears uniforms to school . . . except Steve and me. Instead of their usual blue shirt and plaid bottoms, the kids wear dressy tops and silk bloomer pants in every imaginable color. Teachers take full advantage of the opportunity for personal expression, and the campus is a veritable fashion show of regional Thai design. Steve and I have been looking for Thai clothes for months but without success (or in Steve's case, without enthusiasm), so we wear our usual orange.

The jackets fit great. They make me realize that we never did visit the Hmong, or the Ahka, Karen, or any of the hill tribes of northern Thailand. If we had ended up teaching in a more remote province than Pathum Thani, our sojourn in Thailand would have been completely different. Our living arrangements might have been more rustic, without hot water or air conditioning. We'd probably be in a public school instead of an English-immersion private school. Out of necessity, we might have learned to speak Thai slightly better. All in all, it might have been a more authentically Thai experience.

We would have been far from a city and would never have come to know Bangkok's neighborhoods and landmarks. As Steve will readily admit, and as I will grudgingly concede, our getaways to Bangkok have been our lifeline. At heart, we are city people, and the comforts and culture of the capital have made the stresses of the classroom tolerable. Our daughter Rose was right. I may have wanted an adventure, but coffee shops and yoga studios matter to me. I honestly doubt I would have stuck it out in a more remote corner of the kingdom.

Octopi are beautiful, playful, creative, and intelligent

creatures, but what I find most inspiring is their capacity to change. Like kaleidoscopes, they morph colors and patterns to blend in or stand out. They seem infinitely elastic, squeezing into tiny spaces, stretching to confront threats, and reaching out to touch the world around them. Adapting, shape-shifting, exploring. The octopus embodies my aspirational vision for retirement.

At sixty-one, shape-shifting isn't easy. I'm not a different person now from the one who came to Thailand last October. But I've done a little exploring and have managed to adapt a bit. Tomorrow I'll turn my inner kaleidoscope and change from orange to blue. I'll start to say goodbye to golden marigolds, saffron-robed monks, and the sun blazing in hazy Thai skies. I'll start thinking of home, maybe with a hint of the blues.

Circle Time

The day has flown by, as days with children do, especially when those days are numbered. Now we have just one last circle time, followed by one last dismissal, on our last Friday at Pathum Thani Prep.

Miranda is deviating from the usual departure routine. Too bad. I've grown to love the daily ritual when we all gather at the orange circle and sing our goodbye songs. The sweetest moment is when the kids stand and bow to each teacher, one by one. Whatever mischief makings, attention deficits, squabbles, or runny noses might have frustrated my best attempts to teach, this quiet show of respect at the end of the day cleans the slate. With a serious *wai*, a shining smile, and a "Thank you and goodbye, Teacher Dian," all is forgiven.

"Ivy, why don't you go first? Stand up, please," Miranda prompts. "Tell Teacher Steve and Teacher Dian what fun thing you learned with them." I love Ivy, the oldest girl in a class where boys outnumber girls ten to four. She's got spunk, even more of it now than when we met that first morning assembly last October.

Ivy pops up, walks to the center of the circle, and without hesitation says, "Teacher Dian taught us to make pumpkin pie. It was yummy!" So, our little Thanksgiving celebration made an impression. Back home, my sister is our family's legendary cook and baker. Wait till she hears that here in Pathum Thani I'm the pie lady.

Ivy's enthusiasm inspires Sai—these days, everything Ivy does inspires Sai—who remembers the scent of cinnamon and how taking a big whiff made her sneeze. This apparently gets Chet's mouth watering, and he starts a chant of "Pumpkin pie! Pumpkin pie!" that the rest of the boys join with glee. It's wonderful to see Chet, who is so easily troubled by the world, laughing with his friends, and I'm glad I'll have this memory of one of Pathum Thani's gentlest souls.

After calming the class—I still don't understand how she manages this with such ease—Miranda calls on the oldest of the boys.

"Golf, your turn," says Miranda.

Golf begins, "Teacher Steve taught us about volcanoes and tsunamis, and all the different kinds of whales and sharks, and the tallest buildings, and the biggest cities, and…"

I can't keep from laughing. Golf, whose fifth birthday we celebrated a few weeks ago, is already a human encyclopedia but with a hunger for facts that none of us is ever able to satisfy.

"Golf," Steve interrupts, "I think *you* taught *me* a lot of those things. Thank you for your help!"

Next is Chompoo, the youngest, and maybe the cleverest, in the class. She stands up, considers, and announces, "Teacher Dian taught me to do buttons."

The day I got the little ones to begin to dress themselves was a big day for me. That it was a big event in Chompoo's world touches me more deeply than I would have imagined.

"And then you taught Panit, didn't you?" I say, and Chompoo nods in agreement. I manage to get out, "I'm very proud of both of you." I guess Chompoo, ever an observant child, hears the choke in my voice, because she spreads her tiny arms wide and steps forward for a hug.

Miranda rescues the moment. "Athit, would you like to be next?" she asks.

"No," Athit replies. My sentimentality vanishes, and I can't suppress a snort. Steve just sighs. Neither of us was able to rise to the challenge of this child, but Athit was Steve's particular problem. We wait a beat.

"No, thank you," he corrects himself. I guess he *has* learned a thing or two from us.

After the children leave, Steve and I get to work cleaning out our shared desk. We leave a few items our replacement might find useful, mostly stuff we brought with us from home and don't expect ever to need again: star stickers, an English-Thai dictionary (we still can't read the Thai letters), and some spare facemasks for unhealthy air days.

We organize our collection of story time books, mainly classic American children's literature, in a bookcase. We spent hours reading to the kids. I hope the other teachers noticed how much they enjoyed story time and will pick up where we left off.

It's not quite quitting time yet, so, to keep busy and avoid a prolonged parting scene with the other teachers, we sit in the purple chairs and begin sharpening colored pencils one last time. Miranda and Candace each take a container of pencils and join us at the table.

"Thank you for the circle time today," I say. "It really meant a lot. It's so rare to find out what people remember about you, isn't it?"

"But we aren't finished," says Miranda. "You taught me some things, too. For example, about story time, Steve. The way you read to the kids, asking them what they see in the pictures and what might be coming next. They loved it. I'm going to try, too."

"Oh, it's no great talent," Steve tells her. "All you need is a good book and time." He nods in the direction of the bookcase with our little library.

"You're not taking them home? You might need them. What if you have a grandchild soon?" Miranda asks.

"Don't count your chickens," Steve says to me, which makes no sense to Miranda, which leads us to a short English lesson and an even shorter discussion of our daughter's engagement. We don't bother telling Miranda how easily, and cheaply, we can find books for kids in libraries and at yard sales back home. Here, they are minor treasures. I just hope they'll be put to use, not put on a high shelf to protect them from little hands.

Then Candace begins, "I know teaching in Thailand wasn't your first choice. Neither was kindergarten. But you guys stuck it out—you worked with us. I admire that. And you worked with each other. Your partnership—it's inspiring."

Now this is getting a little more uncomfortable. Not enough time has yet passed to smooth the rough edges of our classroom experience. But she's right. We did stick it out. Once we adopted our AOPG attitude, once we accepted that Miranda and Candace had more experience and were more culturally attuned, we could let them call the shots. These young women are partners, too. They have been the backbone of Prep from its very first day, and they've seen other teachers, like us, come and go.

We hug. We thank one another. We promise to keep in touch, and I think we will. In the short term, we'll have plenty to talk about. How many new children will enroll, and will there be a K3 class next year for Golf, Chet, Ivy, and the rest? Oh, and what about the coronavirus?

We all walk through the playground to the school gate.

Pretending to have forgotten something in the classroom, I go back to slip notes into each of the kids' cubbies. On yellow paper, in neat printing, I've written to Chet, "You are my sunshine," and stuck yellow smiley faces in all the corners. Sai's note tells her "You are very special," with unicorn stickers. For Athit, all I could think of was "Good luck." Then it's goodbye for real.

We hug again, and I squeeze tighter this time, because I know that, in the long term, we might *not* keep in touch. My whole life has been a string of encounters that led to connections and then friendships, followed by separations and promises to stay close, then drifting apart. Occasionally, there has been a drifting back together, but mostly we lose touch. I can't tell you where my third-grade playmates live today, whether my first college roommate ever graduated, or even what some of my longtime colleagues are doing in retirement. I'm not happy about this, but I accept it. Like the octopus, I'm not a social creature. But unlike the octopus, I have a partner.

As Steve and I cross the *soi*, I ask, "So, mission accomplished?"

"Don't count your chickens before they're hatched. We're not home yet," he says.

Trying for my most beautiful *wai*, I put my hands together, bow my head, and say, "Thanks for the adventure."

Wai Thailand

The *soi* is quiet early on Saturday morning—Leap Day, aptly enough. Steve is looking for Tarlo for a final farewell, while I find Pee Wee in the alley. As usual, she has been sweeping the leaves since before sunrise. So as not to startle her, I jangle the dorm keys in the air. The tinkling inspires a potential lesson plan—making wind chimes from old keys, metal washers, and other bits of hardware. Next time. If there ever is a next time.

"*Sawaddee kha,*" Pee Wee says, and I return the hello. Then, with an awkward breaststroke, followed by crisscrossed forearms, she mimes, "Not swimming today?"

I shake my head no, hand her the keys, and say, *"Khop khun kha,"* to thank her for all the mornings she has unlocked the pool gate for us. She understands that we are departing, smiles sweetly, performs a deep *wai*, and repeats, *"Sawaddee kha."* This time, her words mean goodbye.

I don't ask for a going-away photo; that's not my style. But I know that the image of this sturdy, dependable, thoughtful woman will remain with me for a long time to come.

We reach Bangkok in record time—Saturday morning traffic is a fraction of what we've experienced so many times during our Friday afternoon rush hour escapes from Pathum Thani. We spend our final night in Thailand back at the Riverside Hotel, where we are welcomed again with butterfly pea flower tea, whose purple hue coordinates well with the greeter's blue surgical facemask.

On Sunday morning we indulge in one final decadent buffet brunch. I suspect that buffets will soon be a thing of the past, not just here, where they are truly destination dining, but all over the world. Steve checks the airline schedule hourly, because many departures from Bangkok are being canceled. But we are lucky, and on Sunday afternoon we are on a flight home.

When we land in Washington, it's chilly. A light rain is falling. After five months of Thailand's dry season, how wonderful that feels.

Meditation

We sang many songs at Pathum Thani Prep, but the one I love best was the meditation that we sang each morning after raising the Thai flag on the playground. It was the song I sang in Lumphini Park with the keen-eyed young naturalist who was fond of turtles. It is the song that someday I might sing to a grandchild. It is the song that captures my experience of Thailand.

> *I'm breathing in*
> A deep breath and a leap
> *I'm breathing out*
> Into the unknown
> *As flowers bloom*
> Children blossom, teachers grow
> *The mountains high*
> Challenges to overcome or simply accept
> *The rivers sigh*
> Frustration or fulfillment
> *The air that I breathe*
> Transformed
> *I fly*

Epilogue

A few days after our return to Washington we visit my mother in Massachusetts. I resist the powerful urge to wrap my arms around her for fear we've brought the coronavirus from Thailand. Maybe she's leaning a bit more heavily on her walker, but otherwise she looks pretty much the same as when we said goodbye last September. She promised she'd be fine while we were away, and she's been true to her word. But within days, her senior living community will close its doors to visitors, and we won't be allowed back for months.

Twelve confirmed cases of Covid-19 in New York City put the kibosh on our planned visit with Rose and Elliot. We won't see them until summer when we gather for a picnic at a park in New Jersey and meet Rose's future in-laws.

We reconnect with friends and relatives by phone to maintain "social distance." In public and in private, no one embraces or shakes hands. Instead, some Americans bump elbows or mime hugs. We go for walks and teach the neighbors we encounter the Thai *wai*.

Only essential businesses are open, but we can manage without health clubs, hair salons, and happy hours. Toilet paper shortages are front-page news, but we've learned to do without. We're nostalgic for our Pathum Thani bum gun.

Around the world, schools close. By summer the coronavirus rages like wildfire across the United States. It's unclear whether American students will return to class in the fall. But Thai schools reopen in July. We see photos of our kindergartners on social media posts. Their school uniforms now include masks and face shields.

The first detected case of coronavirus outside China was in Thailand, but the epidemic is not out of control there. Scientists don't understand why. Maybe the widespread use of masks, maybe the tradition of the *wai*, kept germs from spreading. Or maybe it is simply good genes or good karma.

We've brought some good karma back with us. Our experience in Thailand was a far cry from what I had envisioned a year ago when I dreamed of teaching abroad. Our biggest challenge was to put those fantasies aside and deal with the reality of Pathum Thani and our classroom. Our return home also fell short of expectations. The constant togetherness we experienced in Thailand was an anomaly in our thirty-year marriage, and Steve and I both looked forward to regaining our independence.

But now, with most normal activities suspended, we spend every day together once again. We rarely leave home. We have time to remember Pathum Thani and to recognize that those months of togetherness were a blessing. They showed us that we make a pretty decent team. They prepared us for the pandemic and for another time, perhaps in the not too distant future, when togetherness might be our only option. And they taught us the wisdom of *mai pen rai*, the wisdom of going with the flow, wherever the flow may be going.

Steve and I are not in touch with our students. Some days, I dream of returning to Thailand and looking them up. I picture a class reunion. In ten years' time, our kids will be teenagers.

Panit will excel at sports, maybe *muay thai*, and I feel sorry for any boxer on the receiving end of his kick. I hope he and Chompoo are still friends. I imagine her keeping a journal, writing about everything she notices and everything she dreams. I worry about Sai and about Athit, but perhaps she is stronger now, and perhaps he has banished whatever demons made him so unhappy.

Golf will surely be at the top of his class, maybe even a grade or two ahead of the others. Will he and all the boys be ordaining as monks? Will any of them keep wearing the orange robes more than the standard couple of months of the rainy season? Chet, perhaps?

Will any of them have to serve in the military, or are their families well enough connected to avoid it? Who will be involved in the Thai democracy movement? I have high hopes for Ivy as a youth leader. Something about Ivy was always looking to the future.

I look to the future, and it's hard. The world these children will inherit will challenge them in ways I don't even want to consider. I hope Steve and I taught them something, anything, that will help them make their way.

Or maybe it's not so hard. They've taught us how to take a deep breath and face a challenge. Maybe they already know how to cope. Maybe *mai pen rai*.

Appendices

Top Ten Things to Do in Thailand
If You Aren't a Tourist

Headed to Thailand for vacation? Lucky you! Read *Lonely Planet*, *Fodor's*, *Frommer's*, or any other travel guide and, by all means, take in their recommended top picks. Bangkok's Grand Palace, Koh Samui's beaches, and Chiang Mai's Elephant Nature Park will not disappoint. But if you're a *farang* sojourning in Thailand, you'll want more than a checklist of photogenic sites. You'll want experiences that nourish your mind, body, and soul.

When Steve and I were teachers in Pathum Thani in 2019–2020, we spent our weekends exploring Bangkok and its environs. Here are my top ten Thai experiences.

1. **Visit the Museum Siam.** If you like the way the Smithsonian's National Museum of American History explains American society, you'll appreciate Museum Siam's take on Thai-ness. Exploring everything from pop culture to national identity, from clothing to language, this Bangkok museum is a great place to begin your Thai adventure and get an inkling of what makes Thailand tick.

2. **Get a Thai massage.** Actually, get many. Weekly sessions worked for us. Your body will thank you and your wallet won't complain, either. Avoid the studio run by Wat Pho Traditional Thai Massage School. While it's the Harvard of training programs, it's touristy, pricey, and inconveniently located. Instead, find a storefront massage studio with a posted menu of services. If you're a newbie, ask for a thirty-minute Thai massage. Next time, you'll go for an

hour-long session. You wear a loose-fitting outfit, provided by the studio, so there's no need to be shy. First, you get a warm footbath, then you lie on a cushion on the floor, close your eyes, and let the therapist perform what you'll come to learn is a rather choreographed set of moves. Thai massage combines deep pressure (like shiatsu) with facilitated stretches (like yoga) and a bit of energy work (like Reiki). You'll walk out feeling like you've just had a great gym workout, but that someone else did all the working out for you! (Note: If you're seeking a massage "with benefits," you can easily find it, but that's not traditional Thai massage.)

3. **Eat Thai street food.** Fearlessly. Everywhere. You might not be able to identify everything you eat, but you'll be amazed by the aromas, textures, and tastes. Thai cooks create complex flavor profiles that combine sweet, salty, sour, and spicy. And more spicy. Thai people love chili peppers, so learn to say *"mai ped"* if, like me, you can't take the heat. Though you may not see a refrigerator or a sink nearby, you don't need to fret about food safety. Freshness is the hallmark of Thai cuisine. We took boxes of Pepto-Bismol to Thailand but didn't use a single tablet.

4. **Ride the public ferries on the Chao Phraya River in Bangkok.** Bangkok's modern, efficient mass transit system is wonderful for getting around the main business and shopping areas of the capital. But to see the national treasures along the riverfront in their full glory, the colorful public ferries are quicker, cheaper, and much more fun.

5. **Eat, drink, love mangoes.** At home, I find tropical fruits sickly sweet, pulpy, and generally unappealing. But in Thailand, they are wonderfully refreshing and delicious. The variety of flavors, colors, and shapes is overwhelming, but to

me, the taste of mango is the taste of Thailand. We ate them, unadorned, most days for breakfast and never grew tired of them. We drank icy mango smoothies as snacks and with meals. Thailand's best dessert has to be mango with sticky rice and coconut cream. Indulge.

6. **Join a *muay thai* gym, and use it!** To be honest, we weren't able to do this in Pathum Thani, but, based on one workout at one gym, I wish we could have. Muay Thai is kickboxing, but it's kickboxing with style. And it's a great workout.

7. **Swim.** I like to bike, and Steve likes to run, but Thailand's chaotic traffic and oppressive heat made these outdoor activities seem like health hazards. Swimming, on the other hand, was a real treat. If you can find a pool, or you're lucky enough to be near the sea, swim.

8. **Hang out at the Bangkok Art and Culture Centre.** This modern ten-story cylindrical structure looks a bit like the Guggenheim in New York and the Hirshhorn in Washington, but it's much more than an art museum. With performance spaces, studios, galleries, bookstores, craft shops, boutiques, cafés, and eateries, it's a great place to people watch and soak up contemporary Thai culture.

9. **Get out of Bangkok.** These unique sites are easy day trips from the capital:

   • Ayutthaya—The ruins of one of Siam's ancient capitals, with Khmer-style architecture, is a UNESCO World Heritage Centre.

   • MOCA Bangkok—The Museum of Contemporary Art is actually in Pathum Thani and features the best of contemporary Thai fine art.

   • National Geological Museum—Also in Pathum Thani, this is a modern museum with a terrific dinosaur exhibit, including the local species *Siamosaurus*. Great for kids.

- Wat Phra Dhammakaya—Another Pathum Thani destination, Thailand's largest Buddhist temple is famous for its million golden Buddha statues.

10. **Visit Wat Pho.** I stand by tip 2, but eventually you'll visit Wat Pho, the Temple of the Reclining Buddha, a must-see cultural icon. While you're there, if you've become as addicted to Thai massage as I did, you'll want to see what all the fuss is about at the famous massage school. Around the temple complex, you'll marvel at the statuary depicting amazingly flexible people in incredible poses, some of which you might experience when you get your massage.

11. **Revisit the Museum Siam.** Yes, I promised my top ten, but I hope you'll treat yourself to one more trip to the Museum Siam before you leave Thailand. Congratulate yourself on how much more you understand about Thailand than when you first arrived. And be humbled by how much you still find a bit unexpected, somewhat enigmatic, or completely inexplicable.

Glossary

Thai Words

amerigaa America. The phrase *prathet amerigaa* refers to the country, as *prathet thai* refers to Thailand.

aroi mak mak It's very delicious. Use this phrase to show appreciation for any Thai food or drink, from a sip of coconut water straight from the shell to a complex preparation that perfectly blends sweet, salty, fishy, spicy, and creamy elements—a hallmark of Thai cuisine.

baht Thai currency. In 2019–2020, the baht was worth about three US cents.

farang A foreigner, specifically a Westerner. I've read that Thai people look down on *farangs*, but if that is true they do an excellent job of hiding it. Not once did I ever feel discriminated against or disrespected as a *farang* in Thailand.

gin khao mai Are you hungry? Or literally, do you want to eat rice? In Thailand, a meal without rice is like a day without sunshine.

goong Shrimp.

hoi tod Oyster (or mussel) omelet, cooked in hot oil and served with chili sauce.

kha Feminine polite particle. By adding this little word to the end of almost any sentence, a woman shows respect for others and for Thai customs, even if she has completely mangled the rest of the sentence. (See *khrap*.)

khao soi Literally, cut rice. A coconut curry soup with rice noodles prepared two ways, boiled and fried, often with chicken, popular in northern Thailand.

khao pad sapparod Pineapple fried rice, seasoned with curry powder and fish sauce, served in a hollowed pineapple shell.

khop khun Thank you. Generally followed by *kha* or *khrap*.

khun A title of respect, preceding a person's given name (or in lieu of a person's name if you don't know it), used for both males and females, regardless of marital status.

khrap Masculine polite particle, corresponding to the feminine *kha*.

khru Teacher. Used both as a job title and, when followed by a teacher's first name, as a form of address.

Loy Krathong Literally, floating (*loy*) basket (*krathong*). A Thai holiday, celebrated on the November full moon.

mai dai Can not. The phrase can mean I (you/he/she/we/they) cannot do something, or that something is prohibited. Expect this response to any unusual request, but don't give up immediately. Often, all you need to change a *mai dai* to a *dai* is a smile and a calm demeanor.

mai khao jai I (you/he/she/we/they) don't understand. Add the appropriate polite particle (*kha* or *khrap*) and a smile, and you will likely be immediately forgiven for your ignorance of the Thai language and congratulated on your ability to articulate that ignorance.

mai mee Don't have. Expect to hear this phrase a lot at eateries. Menus might offer a tempting variety of dishes, but chefs often lack the ingredients to prepare them all.

mai ped Not spicy. This is a critical survival phrase for eating in Thailand. Chilies are to Thai cooking what olive oil is to the Mediterranean diet. If you can't take the heat, these two words are lifesavers.

mai pen rai No problem, it's fine, you're welcome, don't worry. This phrase has lots of uses, and it really does sum up the Thai approach to life. There's no need to fret about anything, because there's not much you can do to change things anyway.

Makha Bucha One of four major Buddhist holidays, Makha Bucha is celebrated on the full moon of the third month of the lunar year, usually in February.

moo ping Grilled pork.

muay thai Thai boxing, the national sport.

nam pla Fish (*pla*) water (*nam*). A salty sauce made from fermented fish and shellfish, used in many Thai dishes.

nidnoy A little bit.

pad thai Stir-fried rice noodles with bean sprouts, peanuts, egg, and other ingredients. Literally, Thai fry.

pee A title meaning older brother or older sister, used to show affection and respect to someone older than the speaker, even if the age difference is very small. The younger person is addressed as *nong*.

raan ah haan Restaurant. Literally, a food shop.

Ramakien The Thai version of the Hindu Ramayana, the legend of the hero Rama, after whom the kings of the current Thai dynasty are named.

rong rian School. Pathum Thani Prep is a school within a school, an English-immersion kindergarten within a much larger elementary school, which I refer to as the *rong rian*.

sawaddee An all-purpose greeting and farewell, often accompanied by a *wai* and a smile. Use the polite particle *kha* or *khrap* afterward to make a good impression.

soi A side street or alleyway.

som tum Green papaya salad. Literally, sour (*som*) pound (*tum*), because unripe papaya is a main ingredient, and the seasonings are mashed and mixed with a mortar and pestle.

Songkran The April 13–15 Thai New Year celebration featuring ritual cleansings and giant outdoor water fights.

tom yum Spicy soup, often served with shrimp (*tom yum goong*). *Tom* means "boil." *Yum* means "mix" and refers to the broth's special combination of sweet, sour, and spicy flavors, which is also used in distinctively Thai versions of potato chips, pretzels, dried seaweed, and other snack foods.

wai The quintessentially Thai form of greeting and showing respect, with the palms joined in front of the chest or face and a bow of the upper body. The exact placement of the hands and the depth of the bow depend on the relative status of the person performing the *wai* and the recipient. A lower-status person offers a *wai* to one of higher status, who might or might not return it. The intricacies of the Thai *wai* are beyond the scope of this glossary, and well beyond the grasp of this author.

wat A Buddhist temple, inhabited and tended by monks, often with a steeply pitched tiled roof and gold embellishments.

Wat Arun The Temple of the Dawn, on the west bank of the Chao Phraya River in Bangkok.

Wat Phrathat Doi Suthep A temple, said to house relics of the Buddha, on a mountain west of Chiang Mai in northern Thailand.

Wat Pho The Temple of the Reclining Buddha, on the east bank of the Chao Phraya River in Bangkok.

Words from Other Languages

auf Wiedersehen (German) Goodbye.

gey gezunt (Yiddish) Goodbye. Go in good health. (See *zai gezunt.*)

la bella lingua (Italian) The beautiful language. (Italian, according to the Italians.)

laoshi (Chinese) Teacher. Form of address for Chinese-language teachers at Pathum Thani Prep.

mensch (Yiddish) A good person, a person of integrity, a dependable person. Definitely, the kind of person you'd want as a son-in-law.

pommes dauphinoise (French) Scalloped potatoes baked with butter and cream.

shtetl (Yiddish) Village.

Siamosaurus, Siamotyrannus (Latin) Siamese lizard and Siamese tyrant, respectively. Two genera of dinosaurs from the Early Cretaceous period.

zai gezunt (Yiddish) Goodbye. Stay in good health. And with this wish to you, Gentle Reader, I end my story.

Acknowledgments

Writing is a solitary endeavor, but creating a book takes a team. I'm grateful to many wonderful people whose expertise, creativity, and moral support helped make this book a reality.

First and foremost is my husband, Steve. We took every step of our Thailand adventure together, and there would be no story to tell without him. When it came time to write, Steve was my touchstone, helping me remember and reconsider events and relationships. I cannot imagine any better companion in Thailand or in life.

There would be no story to tell without our colleagues in Thailand, either. Without the support of our coteachers, our school director, her husband, and our dorm mates, we wouldn't have survived kindergarten. Their friendship meant the world to me.

I thank all the friends and family members who read the *Missives from Thailand* we sent each month and encouraged me to write a book. Did they really think I'd take their enthusiasm to heart? Special shout-outs to the beach crowd in Margate, my girl gang from Marblehead, and all my book club friends.

Supportive early readers gave me much-needed criticism generously sandwiched between slices of praise and encouragement. My heartfelt thanks to Jennie Bauduy, Olga Doty, Britteny Hudson, Peggi Hunter, Bob Matthews, Denise McAllister, Nancy Prendergast, Trudy Todd, and Cathy Wu for slogging through rough-and-tumble drafts and helping me revise, revise, revise.

I am forever grateful to Developmental Editors Lynn Auld Schwartz (Writer's Wordhouse) and Laura Oliver (The Story

Within) for helping me find my story and tell it well and to Katherine Pickett (POP Editorial Services) for meticulously copyediting the final manuscript.

I offer a respectful *wai* and heartfelt *khop khun kha* to Rattanawali Brodsley (Aom) and Varavejbhisis Yossiri for bringing their expertise in Thai culture and language to this book and helping me understand their homeland a little better. My gratitude to Jessie Glenn and the Mindbuck Media publicity team for their expertise, creativity, and support.

A huge thank-you to the students of Loyola University Maryland who staff Apprentice House Press, and its director, Dr. Kevin Atticks. I could not have asked for a more engaged editorial and production team. Being part of their education in publishing has been an honor and a joy. I'm especially grateful to Acquisitions and Developmental Editor Cat Cusma for believing in this story and helping improve it, to Sienna Whelan for designing the map of Thailand, to April Hartman for the interior and cover designs, and to Corrine Moulds who managed the team.

Special thanks to the Writer's Center in Bethesda, Maryland, where I found teachers, editors, and critique groups that became the foundation of my writing community. Around the corner, the friendly staff and yummy lunches at the Thai Kitchen helped conjure memories of Thailand as this book took shape.

Finally, I thank a microscopic novel coronavirus that made its presence known during our final months in Thailand. Though it wreaked havoc on human civilization and caused untold misery, Covid-19 kept me indoors, at my laptop, and plugging away at this book for the better part of two years. The pandemic taught me that when life hands you lemons, maybe you try writing about mangoes.

About the Author

Before her unexpected "second act" teaching kindergarten in Thailand, Dian Seidel was a climate scientist at the National Oceanic and Atmospheric Administration. Her research contributed to the 2007 Nobel Peace Prize-winning Intergovernmental Panel on Climate Change. Originally from Massachusetts, she now lives in the Washington, DC, area, where she teaches English as a second language and Iyengar yoga. Her writing has appeared in *Passager, Anak Sastra, Lucky Jefferson, Pen in Hand, The New York Times,* and *Bethesda Magazine.* She loves crossword puzzles, book clubs, open ocean swimming, and the heart of a ripe watermelon on an August afternoon.

Visit her at www.DianSeidel.com.

Apprentice House Press

Loyola University Maryland

Apprentice House Press is the country's only campus-based, student-staffed book publishing company. Directed by professors and industry professionals, it is a nonprofit activity of the Communication Department at Loyola University Maryland.

Using state-of-the-art technology and an experiential learning model of education, Apprentice House publishes books in untraditional ways. This dual responsibility as publishers and educators creates an unprecedented collaborative environment among faculty and students, while teaching tomorrow's editors, designers, and marketers.

Eclectic and provocative, Apprentice House titles intend to entertain as well as spark dialogue on a variety of topics. Financial contributions to sustain the press's work are welcomed. Contributions are tax deductible to the fullest extent allowed by the IRS.

To learn more about Apprentice House books or to obtain submission guidelines, please visit www.apprenticehouse.com.

Apprentice House Press
Communication Department
Loyola University Maryland
4501 N. Charles Street
Baltimore, MD 21210
Ph: 410-617-5265
info@apprenticehouse.com • www.apprenticehouse.com